Need More than Reference Help?

APA Made Easy for up to 30% Off

As a thank you for supporting this book, go to www.YouVersusTheWorld.com to purchase APA Made Easy for 20% off the Amazon.com list price. Enter coupon code "**Ref20%off**".

Share your purchase on facebook or Twitter and get another 10% off!

OVER 10,000 COPIES SOLD

APA

MADE EASY

3RD EDITION | UPDATED AND EXPANDED

SCOTT MATKOVICH

What is APA Made Easy?

We believe that no student should have to spend more than 15 minutes formatting their papers.

Whether you want a step-by-step guide to building a title page, suggestions for writing with greater clarity, or freedom from doing internet searches every time you have a question about APA standards, APA Made Easy is the only blueprint that you will need for writing in APA style. This comprehensive writing guide includes illustrated steps for formatting an APA document in: Microsoft Word 2010, Microsoft Word 2011 for Mac, Microsoft Word 2013, and Apple's Pages programs. You will also learn:

- How to organize an essay or research paper.
- Steps for writing an essay with greater clarity and precision.
- How to write an essay or research paper from an outline.
- Numerous APA examples and high resolution screen shots to help students correctly format documents within 15 minutes.
- Tips for adding clarity to any writing style including:How to write your paper with greater "flow" of thought and a Quick Reference guide for writing coherence.
- A new section on using and citing DOI's (Digital Object Identifiers) for new media.

Table of Contents

All of the information in this book is in accordance with the Publication Manual of the American Psychological Association, Sixth Edition

A Guide for Building Any Reference

If there is any part of APA formatting that students struggle with the most, it is their reference sheet. After much weeping and gnashing of teeth, I have decided to organize the reference section of this book in the order that the references are built - from left to right.

Formatting Note: One limitation in producing a book like this is formatting hanging indents. In APA format, all references that are longer than the first line should be indented and double spaced. I recognize that the examples throughout this book do not follow that format. Always be sure to indent the second, third, etc. lines of your references.

- **Author and Editor Names**
- **Date of Publication**
- **Name of Article (if needed)**
- **Title of Reference**
- **Location**
- **Name of Publisher**

In this section, I will explain each section of an APA reference in more detail than you probably care to read - but it's there if you need it. If you wish to skip all the explanations and look directly at samples for over 30 references, skip to the completed references examples given at the end of this section. If you would like a more visual representation of the same information below, visit my website, where I am compiling examples of all kinds APA references.

Formatting Author and Editor Names:

With a few exceptions, the first thing we write when referencing a resources is the author or editor names. The author or authors last name is written first with a comma, then their first initial with a period. For example an author with the name John Anders would be written like this:

Anders, J.

For two authors, the same practice works by writing their names in the order they appear in the book (usually alphabetical, but not necessarily) - separating the names with an ampersand (&). For example:

Anders, J. & Bieler, R.

For three to seven authors:

List the authors by last name, separating each name with a comma. When you get to the last author, place an ampersand (&) symbol *before* their name. For example:

Anders, J., Bieler, R., Johnson, L., & White, B.

If you are using a book that has an editor or editors, their names are used in this section as well. For a single editor, follow the author formula above and simply add (Ed.). or (Eds.). after the editor's first name initial. For example:

Anders, J. (Ed.).

For multiple editors:

Anders, J. & Bieler, R. (Eds.).
Anders, J., Bieler, R., Johnson, L., & White, B. (Eds.).

For publications that list corporations, organizations, governments as the author, write the organization name as it is printed *without* abbreviating any part of the name. For example:

Department of Education. (2013). *The education in America.* Salem: OR. Anchor Press.

Specifically, for publications classified as Online Encyclopedias, Journal Article with No Author, and Magazine Article with No Author, the name of the article is placed where the author name would usually go. For example, the full reference for an online encyclopedia would look like this:

Speed of Light. (n.d.). In *The Encyclopedia Britannica* (Vol. 8, pp. 218-219). Retrieved from http://www.encyclopediabrittanica.com

Formatting the Date of Publication:

The date of publication is placed after the author or editor name. When formatting our references for the date of publication, we will primarily use three different formats - depending on the kind of reference. Regardless of the format, the date of publication is always placed inside of parentheses.

The *most common* format for the date of publication is the year of publication inside of a parenthesis. This is how it will appear next to an author's name:

Anders, J. (2013).

Use this format for the following references:

- Book with One Author
- Book with Multiple Authors
- Edited Book with No Authors
- Edited Book with an Author or Authors
- Edition of Book Other than the First Edition
- Multivolume Work
- Encyclopedia Entry
- E-book (if a date of publication is given)
- Online Encyclopedia

- Online Lecture Notes and Presentation Slides
- Web Page
- Computer Software
- Journal Article
- Journal Article with no Author (if a date of publication is given)
- Chapter from an Online Article or E-book

Another way to format the date of publication is to insert the year of publication, then the month and date. As compared with the references above which are more traditional, this format is primarily used for references related to articles or blog posts. For example, a newspaper article reference would look like this:

Anders, J. (2013, May 6). APA rules. *The Denver Post.* Retrieved from http://www.denverpost.com

Notice how both the year and the month and day are written. Use this format for the following references:

- Newspaper Article
- Blog
- Audio Podcast
- Online Forum or Discussion Board
- Online Magazine Article
- Magazine Article with No Author
- Online Book Reviews

Finally, (n.d.). stands for no date, is used in cases where a reference does not have a date of publication associated with it. This format can be used for any reference, though it is most commonly used for online references since publication dates for online articles are not always listed. Here is an example of how this would look for an E-book with no publication date listed:

Anders, J. (n.d.). *APA made easy.* Retrieved from http://www.apamadeeasy.com

If you can find a publication date, you should use it. If you cannot find a publication date, use (n.d.). in this field.

Formatting the Name of Article (If Needed)

If the reference you are citing an article, the name of the article should be a part of your reference. The name of the article follows the date of publication and precedes the title of the publication. Format the name of the article by capitalizing only the first letter of the first word in the name of the article. For example, if we were to cite a Podcast that has an episode name and title, it would look like this:

Anders, J. (2013, May 6). APA rules. Podcast retrieved from http://www.APAMadeEasy.edu/podcast.htm

Of course, this is APA format, it can't be that easy! There are other additions that go in the article field in addition to the article name. Notably, when citing computer hardware, your article field will include: [computer software] in brackets. For example:

Anders, J. (2013). APA rules [computer software]. New York, NY: Anchor Press.

For a blog post:

Anders, J. (2013, May 6). APA rules [Web log comment]. Retrieved from http://www.youversustheworld.com/references

Title of Reference

If the resource you are referencing does not have an article name, the title of the publication will appear after the date of publication. In APA format the title of a publication is always *italicized.*

Special Note on Capitalization: One mistake I see students make surrounds the concept of capitalization. You will notice in the example below that certain titles are capitalized and others are not. Here are the criteria to use when deciding whether or not to capitalize a title:

- Always capitalize all essential words in a journal title.
- Only the first letter of the first word is capitalized when when writing titles for books, articles, chapters, and web pages. If you are referencing a sub-title, capitalize the first letter of the first word as well.
- Proper nouns are *always* capitalized, even in the titles for books, article, chapters, and webpages. A proper noun is a name for a person, place, thing, or idea.
- The first letter of the first word after a colon or dash can be capitalized.

Here is an itemized way of thinking about writing the title of each kind of reference:

Books, E-books, and Newspaper Articles: Simply list and italicize the title of the publication. Only the first letter of the first word is capitalized.

Books with Editions Other than the First: List and italicize the name of the book and write the number of the edition in parentheses.

APA made easy (4th ed.).

A Multivolume Work: List and italicize the title of the reference and write the volume(s) that you used in your paper in parentheses. If you have page numbers available, include them within the parenthesis as well. For a single volume use (Vol.) and for multiple volumes use (Vols.).

APA made easy (Vol. 2).
APA made easy (Vols. 1-3).

For an Encyclopedia Entry or Online Encyclopedia Entry: Write "*In the*" then the encyclopedia title. For example, "In *The Encyclopedia Britannica.*" In parentheses include the volume number(s) and the page numbers that you are referencing. In this particular title, the word "In" is not italicized, nor are the volume and page numbers.

In *The Encyclopedia Britannica* (Vol. 4, pp. 36-85).
In *The Encyclopedia Britannica* online.

Online Lecture Notes and/or Presentation Slides: Italicize the title of the lecture and in brackets note the kind of presentation noted.

APA Made Easy [Powerpoint Document].

Audio Podcast: Italicize and write the title of the Podcast. Afterward, we would write "Podcast retrieved from ..."

APA Made Easy. Podcast Retrieved from *http://www.itunes.com*

Journals, Online Journals, and Journals with no Author: Journals are the anomaly in the reference page. First, we capitalize all essential words. Our first example will be of a journal with an italicized volume number and unitalicized page numbers only:

APA Made Easy, 12, p. 25.

If the journal you are citing has an volume and issue number, the issue number goes after the volume number, unitalicized and in parentheses:

APA Made Easy, 12(4), pp. 15-33.

Magazine Article, Online Magazine Article, Magazine Article with no Author: The title section for a magazine article looks a lot like a journal as it includes the volume and issue numbers, if noted in the magazine. After the volume and or the issue number, the unitalicized page numbers of the reference are included.
For a magazine with a volume number only:

APA Made Easy Magazine, 14, 28-31.

The title of a magazine with a volume number and issue number:

APA Made Easy Magazine, 14(8), 28-31.

Location of Publication

The location section of the reference page notes either where the reference was published (City and State), the website that the reference was published, or a DOI. Because of the popularity of online research, DOI's are becoming increasingly popular. Always include a DOI at the end of your reference if possible.

The standard location for most physical reference materials includes the city and state initial where the reference was published. A comma is entered after the city name and before the state initial. After the state initial include a colon. For example:

New York, NY:

This location format is typical for the following types of references:

- Book with One Author
- Book with Multiple Authors
- Edited Book with No Authors
- Edited Book with an Author or Authors
- Edition of Book Other than the First Edition
- Multivolume Work
- Encyclopedia Entry
- Computer Software

For resources based online, this section of our reference is used to denote where we retrieved the resource from. Typically, we start these location references with the words "Retrieved from". For example, if we are referencing a blog, we write:

Retrieved from http://www.youversustheworld.com/blog

Publisher

For print resources, the publisher is the last section of the reference! Simply list the publisher one space after the colon of the state initial. Write it exactly as it is written in the resource you are referencing and add a period at the end and you are done!

Chapter 1: References for Books

References for Books without an Author or Editor

A Quick Overview : **Books without An Author or Editor**

Sample Reference Structure for a Book without an Author or Editor

Title of book (Edition number, if needed). (Date of Publication). City, State Initials: Publisher.

Example:

APA made easy. (2013). Denver, CO: Anchor Press.

Electronic Sample

Title of book (Edition number, if needed). (Date of Publication). Retrieved from http://nameofurl.com

Electronic Example

APA made easy. (2014). Retrieved from http://www.youversustheworld.com/url

Sample In-Text Citations for a Book without and Author or Editor

Example #1: Paraphrase

According to APA Made Easy (2012), writing in APA format can be easy.

Example #2: Paraphrase

With so many resources available, writing in APA format can be easy ("APA Made Easy," 2012).

Example #3: Direct Quote

APA Made Easy (2012) states, "Writing in APA format can be easy" (p. iv).

Example #4: Direct Quote

With so many resources available, writing in APA format can be easy ("APA Made Easy," 2012, p. 12).

Books without an Author or Editor

Book without an Author, Standard Date

APA made easy. (2013). Denver, CO: Anchor Press.

Book without an Author or Editor, No Date

APA made easy. (n.d.). Denver, CO: Anchor Press.

In Text Citation Example:

(APA Made Easy, n.d.)

Book without an Author or Editor, Edition Other than First

APA made easy (4th ed.). (2013). Denver, CO: Anchor Press.

Book without an Author or Editor, Revised Edition

APA made easy (Rev. ed.). (2013). Denver, CO: Anchor Press.

Book without an Author or Editor, Title with Subtitle

APA made easy: Writing with style. (2012). New York, NY: Anchor Press.

In Text Citation:

(APA Made Easy, 2012)

Book without an Author or Editor, No Date, Title with Subtitle

APA made easy: Writing with style. (n.d.). New York, NY: Anchor Press.

In Text Citation:

(APA Made Easy, n.d.)

Book without an Author or Editor, Title with Series Name

APA made easy: Vol. 4. Writing with style. (2012). New York, NY: Anchor Press.

Book without an Author, Limited Circulation, Not Available Online

Writing with style. (2014). (Available from Baker, 122 S. Salem Street, Billings, MT, 59101)

Book without an Author, Limited Circulation, From Online Database

Writing with style. (2014). Retrieved from http://nameofdatabaseurl.edu/onlinereferences

Book without an Author, Monograph

Writing with style [Monograph]. (2014). Retrieved from http://nameofdatabaseurl.edu/onlinereferences

Non-English Reference Book Translated into English, Entire Book

Seja Feliz. (2014). *Bondade E' A Resposta* [Goodness is the answer] (13th ed.). Mexico City, Mexico: Anchor Press.

Chapter in Book without a Listed Author or Editor

Formatting for fun. (2014). *We write without ceasing* (pp. 91-103). New York, NY: Anchor Press.

Electronic Book/Ebook without an Author

APA made easy. (2014). Retrieved from http://www.youversustheworld.com/ebookwithoutanauthor

Book without an Author, Electronic Book/Ebook of Print Book

Writing with style [Kindle version]. (2014). Retrieved from http://www.youversustheworld.com/asp

Chapter in Electronic Book/Ebook without a Listed Author or Editor

Formatting for fun. (2014). *We write without ceasing* (pp. 91-103). Retrieved from http://www.youversustheworld/chaptertitles

Chapter in Electronic Book/Ebook without a Listed Author or Editor, with DOI

Formatting for fun. (2014). *We write without ceasing* (pp. 91-103). doi: 10.1234567890

Entry in Reference Book without Author or Editor

Formatting for fun. (2014). In *Standard writer's desk dictionary* (2nd ed.). Fort Collins, CO: Anchor Press.

Entry in Online Reference Book without Author or Editor

Formatting for fun. (2014). In *Standard writer's desk dictionary* (2nd ed.). Retrieved from http://www.youversustheworld.com/onlinereferences

Entry in Online Reference Book without Author or Editor, No Date, with DOI

Formatting for fun. (n.d.). In *Standard writer's desk dictionary* (2nd ed.). doi: 10.1234567890

References for Books with No Author, One Editor

A Quick Overview of Formatting Citations and References for **Books with One Editor**

Sample Reference Structure for a Book with One Editor

Editor Last Name, First Initial. (Ed.). (Year of Publication). *Title of Publication.* City, State Initials: Publisher.

Example:

Anders, J. (Ed.). (2013). *APA made easy.* New York, NY: Anchor Press.

Electronic Sample

Editor Last Name, First Initial. (Ed.). (Year of Publication). *Title of Publication.* Retrieved from http://nameofurl.com

Electronic Example

Anders, J. A. (Ed.). (2014). *Writing with style.* Retrieved from http://www.youversustheworld.com/ebookreferences

Sample In-Text Citations for a Book with One Editor

Example #1: Paraphrase

According to a book edited by Anders (2012), writing in APA format can be easy.

Example #2: Paraphrase

With so many resources available, writing in APA format can be easy (Anders, 2012).

Example #3: Direct Quote

Anders (2012) stated, "Writing in APA format can be easy" (p. 8).

Example #4: Direct Quote

"Writing in APA format can be easy" (Anders, 2012, p. 8).

Edited Books with No Author, One Editor

One Editor, No Author, Standard Date

Anders, J. (Ed.). (2013). *APA made easy.* New York, NY: Anchor Press.

One Editor, No Date, No Author

Anders, J. (Ed.). (n.d.). *APA made easy.* New York, NY: Anchor Press.

One Editor, No Author, Republished Version - Use the latest date listed

Anders, J. (Ed.). (2014). *APA made easy.* New York, NY: Anchor Press.

In Text Citation Example - Cite both the original published date and the date of the republished version:
(Anders, 2000/2014).

One Editor, No Author, Edition Other Than First

Anders, J. (Ed.). (2013). *APA made easy* (4th ed.). New York, NY: Anchor Press.

One Editor, No Author, Revised Edition

Anders, J. (Ed.). (2013). *APA made easy* (Rev. ed.). New York, NY: Anchor Press.

One Editor, No Author, Title with Subtitle

Anders, J. (Ed.). (2013). *APA made easy: Writing with style.* New York, NY: Anchor Press.

One Editor, No Author, No Date, Title with Subtitle

Anders, J. (Ed.). (n.d.). *APA made easy: Writing with style.* New York, NY: Anchor Press.

One Editor, No Author, Title with Subtitle, Edition Other Than First

Anders, J. (Ed.). (2013). *APA made easy: Writing with style* (4th ed.). New York, NY: Anchor Press.

One Editor, No Author, Title with Series

Anders, J. (Ed.). (2013). *APA made easy: Vol. 4. Writing with style.* New York, NY: Anchor Press.

One Editor, No Author, Limited Circulation Book, Not Online

Anders, J. A. (Ed.). (2014). *Writing with style: Formatting for fun.* (Available from Baker, 122 South Salem Street, Billings, MT, 59101)

One Editor, No Author, Limited Circulation, From Online Database

Anders, J. A. (Ed.). (2014). *Writing with style: Formatting for fun.* Retrieved from http://www.onlinedatabaseurl.edu/limitedcirculation

One Editor, No Author, Monograph

Anders, J. A. (Ed.). (2014). *Writing with style: Formatting for fun* [Monograph]. Retrieved from http://www.onlinedatabaseurl.edu/limitedcirculation

Non-English Reference Book Translated into English, Entire Book, No Author, with One Editor

Seja Feliz. (2014). In R. Guerrimo *Bondade E' A Resposta* [Goodness is the answer] (13th ed.). Mexico City, Mexico: Anchor Press.

Multivolume Work with One Editor, No Author

Anders, J. R. (Ed.). (2014). *Encyclopedia of Accounting Terms* (Vols. 1-8). Dacono, CO: Anchor Press.

Multivolume Work with One Editor, No Author, Other than First Edition

Anders, J. R. (Ed.). (2014). *Encyclopedia of Accounting Terms* (3rd ed., Vols. 1-8). Dacono, CO: Anchor Press.

One Editor, No Author, Chapter in Book

We format for fun. (2014). In R. Miller (Ed.), *Writing with style* (pp. 91-103). New York, NY: Anchor Press.

One Editor, No Author, Electronic Book/Ebook

Anders, J. A. (Ed.). (2014). *Writing with style.* Retrieved from http://www.youversustheworld.com/ebookreferences

One Editor, No Author, Electronic Version of Print Version (Kindle, Nook, etc.)

Anders, J. C. (Ed.). (2014). *APA made easy* [Kindle DX version]. Retrieved from http://www.youversustheworld.com

One Editor, No Author, Chapter in Electronic Book/Ebook

We format for fun. (2014). In R. Miller (Ed.), *Writing with style* (pp. 91-103). Retrieved from http://www.youversustheworld/bookchapter

One Editor, No Author, Chapter in Electronic Book/Ebook, with DOI

We format for fun. (2014). In R. Miller (Ed.), *Writing with style* (pp. 91-103). doi: 10.1234567890

Reference Book with One Editor, No Author

Anders, J. (Ed.). (2014). *References in obscurity*. Wauconda, IL: Anchor Press.

Entry in Reference Book with One Editor, No Author

References in obscurity. (2014). In R. Miller (Ed.), *Getting references right* (3rd ed., Vol. 8). Wauconda, IL: Anchor Press.

Entry in Online Reference Book with One Editor, No Author

References in obscurity. (2014). In R. Miller (Ed.), *Getting references right* (3rd ed., Vol. 8). Retrieved from http://www.youversustheworld.com/referencesbooks

Entry in Online Reference Book with One Editor, No Author, with DOI

References in obscurity. (2014). In R. Miller (Ed.), *Getting references right* (3rd ed., Vol. 8). doi: 10.1234567890

Entry in Online Reference Book with One Editor, No Author, Alternative Edition Example

References in obscurity. (2014). In R. Miller (Ed.), *Getting references right* (Spring 2008 ed.). Retrieved from http://www.youversustheworld.com/referencesbooks

Multivolume Work with One Editor, Other than First Edition, Online

Anders, J. (Ed.). (2014). *Encyclopedia of Accounting Terms* (3rd ed., Vols. 1-8). Retrieved from http://www.youversustheworld.com/encyclopedia

References for Books with No Author, Two Editors

A Quick Overview : **Books with Two Editors**

Sample Reference Structure for a Book with Two Editors:

Editor Last Name, First Initial., & Second Editor Last Name, First Initial. (Eds.). (Year of Publication). *Title of Publication.* City, State Initials: Publisher.

Example:

Anders, J., & Markol, C. A. (Eds.). (2013). *APA made easy.* New York, NY: Anchor Press.

Electronic Sample

Editor Last Name, First Initial., & Second Editor Last Name, First Initial. (Eds.). (Year of Publication). *Title of Publication.* Retrieved from http://nameofurl.com

Electronic Example

Anders, J., & Markol, C. A. (Eds.). (2013). *APA made easy.* Retrieved from http://www.youversustheworld.com/ebookreferences

Sample In-Text Citations for a Book with Two Editors

Example #1: Paraphrase

According to a book edited by Anders and Beiler's (2012), writing in APA format can be easy.

Example #2: Paraphrase

With so many resources available, writing in APA format can be easy (Anders & Beiler, 2012).

Example #3: Direct Quote

Anders and Beiler (2012) stated, "Writing in APA format can be easy" (p. 8).

Example #4: Direct Quote

With so many resources available, writing in APA format can be easy (Anders & Beiler, 2012, p. 8).

Edited Books with Two Editors, No Author

Two Editors, No Author, Standard Date

Anders, J., & Markol, C. A. (Eds.). (2013). *APA made easy.* New York, NY: Anchor Press.

Two Editors, No Date, No Author

Anders, J., & Markol, C. A. (Eds.). (n.d.). *APA made easy.* New York, NY: Anchor Press.

Two Editors, No Author, Republished Version - Use the latest date listed

Anders, J., & Markol, C. A. (Eds.). (2014). *APA made easy.* New York, NY: Anchor Press.

In Text Citation Example - Cite both the original published date and the date of the republished version:

(Anders & Markol, 2000/2014).

Two Editors, No Author, Edition Other Than First

Anders, J., & Markol, C. A. (Eds.). (2013). *APA made easy* (4th ed.). New York, NY: Anchor Press.

Two Editors, No Author, Revised Edition

Anders, J., & Markol, C. A. (Eds.). (2013). *APA made easy* (Rev. ed.). New York, NY: Anchor Press.

Two Editors, No Author, Title with Subtitle

Anders, J., & Markol, C. A. (Eds.). (2013). *APA made easy: Writing with style.* New York, NY: Anchor Press.

Two Editors, No Author, No Date, Title with Subtitle

Anders, J., & Markol, C. A. (Eds.). (n.d.). *APA made easy: Writing with style.* New York, NY: Anchor Press.

Two Editors, No Author, Title with Subtitle, Edition Other Than First

Anders, J., & Markol, C. A. (Eds.). (2013). *APA made easy: Writing with style* (4th ed.). New York, NY: Anchor Press.

Two Editors, No Author, Title with Series

Anders, J., & Markol, C. A. (Eds.). (2013). *APA made easy: Vol. 4. Writing with style.* New York, NY: Anchor Press.

Two Editors, No Author, Limited Circulation Book, Not Online

Anders, J. A., & Zen, D. (Eds.). (2014). *Writing with style: Formatting for fun.* (Available from Baker, 122 South Salem Street, Billings, MT, 59101)

Two Editors, No Author, Limited Circulation, From Online Database

Anders, J. A., & Zen, D. (Eds.). (2014). *Writing with style: Formatting for fun.* Retrieved from http://www.onlinedatabaseurl.edu/limitedcirculation

Two Editors, No Author, Monograph

Anders, J. A., & Zen, D. (Eds.). (2014). *Writing with style: Formatting for fun* [Monograph]. Retrieved from http://www.onlinedatabaseurl.edu/limitedcirculation

Non-English Reference Book Translated into English, Entire Book, No Author, with Two Editors

Seja Feliz. (2014). In R. Guerrimo *Bondade E' A Resposta* [Goodness is the answer] (13th ed.). Mexico City, Mexico: Anchor Press.

Multivolume Work with Two Editors, No Author

Anders, J. A., & Zen, D. (Eds.). (2014). *Encyclopedia of Accounting Terms* (Vols. 1-8). Dacono, CO: Anchor Press.

Multivolume Work with Two Editors, No Author, Other than First Edition

Anders, J. A., & Zen, D. (Eds.). (2014). *Encyclopedia of Accounting Terms* (3rd ed., Vols. 1-8). Dacono, CO: Anchor Press.

Two Editors, No Author, Chapter in Book

We format for fun. (2014). In R. Miller & J. J. Warfield (Eds.), *Writing with style* (pp. 91-103). New York, NY: Anchor Press.

Two Editors, No Author, Electronic Book/Ebook

Anders, J. A., & Zen, D. (Eds.). (2014). *Writing with style.* Retrieved from http://www.youversustheworld.com/ebookreferences

Two Editors, No Author, Electronic Version of Print Version (Kindle, Nook, etc.)

Anders, J. A., & Zen, D. (Eds.). (2014). *APA made easy* [Kindle DX version]. Retrieved from http://www.youversustheworld.com

Two Editors, No Author, Chapter in Electronic Book/Ebook

We format for fun. (2014). In R. Miller & J. J. Warfield (Eds.), *Writing with style* (pp. 91-103). Retrieved from http://www.youversustheworld/bookchapter

Two Editors, No Author, Chapter in Electronic Book/Ebook, with DOI

We format for fun. (2014). In R. Miller & J. J. Warfield (Eds.), *Writing with style* (pp. 91-103). doi:10.1234567890

Reference Book with Two Editors, No Author

Anders, J., & Markol, C. A. (Eds.). (2014). *References in obscurity.* Wauconda, IL: Anchor Press.

Entry in Reference Book with Two Editors, No Author

References in obscurity. (2014). In R. Miller & J. J. Warfield (Eds.), *Getting references right* (3rd ed., Vol. 8). Wauconda, IL: Anchor Press.

Entry in Online Reference Book with Two Editors, No Author

References in obscurity. (2014). In R. Miller & J. J. Warfield (Eds.), *Getting references right* (3rd ed., Vol. 8). Retrieved from http://www.youversustheworld.com/referencesbooks

Entry in Online Reference Book with Two Editors, No Author, with DOI

References in obscurity. (2014). In R. Miller & J. J. Warfield (Eds.), *Getting references right* (3rd ed., Vol. 8). doi:10.1234567890

Entry in Online Reference Book with Two Editors, No Author, Alternative Edition Example

References in obscurity. (2014). In R. Miller & J. J. Warfield (Eds.), *Getting references right* (Spring 2008 ed.). Retrieved from http://www.youversustheworld.com/referencesbooks

Multivolume Work with Two Editors, Other than First Edition, Online

Anders, J., & Markol, C. A. (Eds.). (2014). *Encyclopedia of Accounting Terms* (3rd ed., Vols. 1-8). Retrieved from http://www.youversustheworld.com/encyclopedia

Contents for Books with No Author, Three Editors

A Quick Overview : **Books with Three Editors**

Sample Reference Structure:

Editor Last Name, First Initial., Second Editor Last Name, First Initial., & Third Author Last Name, First Initial. (Eds.). (Year of Publication). *Title of Publication.* City, State Initials: Publisher.

Example:

Anders, J., Beiler, R., & Markol, C.A. (Eds.). (2013). *APA made easy.* New York, NY: Anchor Press.

Electronic Sample

Editor Last Name, First Initial., Second Editor Last Name, First Initial., & Third Author Last Name, First Initial. (Eds.). (Year of Publication). *Title of Publication.* Retrieved from http://nameofurl.com

Electronic Example

Anders, J., Beiler, R., & Markol, C.A. (Eds.). (2014). *Writing with style.* Retrieved from http://www.youversustheworld.com/ebookreferences

Sample In-Text Citations

For your first time citing a book with three authors, your in text citation should appear like this:
(Smith, Johnson, & Zeigler, 2013)

For subsequent paragraph citation after the first
(Smith et al., 2013)

Every subsequent citation omits the year:
(Smith et al.)

Example #1: Paraphrase

There have been cases where people have compared Smith, Johnson, and Zeigler (2012) to *APA Made Easy* because of the similarities in writing style.

Example #2: Paraphrase

Smith et al. (2012) have compared to APA formatting to MLA formatting.

Example #3: Second Instance of Paraphrase

Smith et al. have compared to APA formatting to MLA formatting.

Example #4: Direct Quote

The book on Fairy Tales was described as "a wonderful tale of hope and dreams" (Smith, Johnson, & Zeigler, 2012, p. 12).

Example #5: Direct Quote, Second Instance

The book on Fairy Tales was described as "a wonderful tale of hope and dreams" (Smith et al., 2012, p. 12).

Edited Books with Three Editors, No Author

Three Editors, Standard Date, No Author

Anders, J., Beiler, R., & Markol, C.A. (Eds.). (2013). *APA made easy.* New York, NY: Anchor Press.

Three Editors, No Date, No Author

Anders, J., Beiler, R., & Markol, C.A. (Eds.). (n.d.). *APA made easy.* New York, NY: Anchor Press.

Three Editors, No Author, Republished Version - Use the latest date listed

Anders, J., Beiler, R., & Markol, C.A. (Eds.). (2014). *APA made easy.* New York, NY: Anchor Press.

In Text Citation Example - Cite both the original published date and the date of the republished version:

(Anders, Beiler, & Markol, 2000/2014).

Three Editors, No Author, Edition Other Than First

Anders, J., Beiler, R., & Markol, C.A. (Eds.). (2013). *APA made easy* (4th ed.). New York, NY: Anchor Press.

Three Editors, No Author, Revised Edition

Anders, J., Beiler, R., & Markol, C.A. (Eds.). (2013). *APA made easy* (Rev. ed.). New York, NY: Anchor Press.

Three Editors, No Author, Title with Subtitle

Anders, J., Beiler, R., & Markol, C.A. (Eds.). (2013). *APA made easy: Writing with style.* New York, NY: Anchor Press.

Three Editors, No Author, No Date, Title with Subtitle

Anders, J., Beiler, R., & Markol, C.A. (Eds.). (n.d.). *APA made easy: Writing with style.* New York, NY: Anchor Press.

Three Editors, No Author, Title with Subtitle, Edition Other Than First

Anders, J., Beiler, R., & Markol, C.A. (Eds.). (2013). *APA made easy: Writing with style* (4th ed.). New York, NY: Anchor Press.

Three Editors, No Author, Title with Series

Anders, J., Beiler, R., & Markol, C.A. (Eds.). (2013). *APA made easy: Vol. 4. Writing with style.* New York, NY: Anchor Press.

Three Editors, No Author, Limited Circulation Book, Not Online

Anders, J., Beiler, R., & Markol, C.A. (Eds.). (2014). *Writing with style: Formatting for fun.* (Available from Baker, 122 South Salem Street, Billings, MT, 59101)

Three Editors, No Author, Limited Circulation, From Online Database

Anders, J., Beiler, R., & Markol, C.A. (Eds.).(2014). *Writing with style: Formatting for fun.* Retrieved from http://www.onlinedatabaseurl.edu/limitedcirculation

Three Editors, No Author, Monograph

Anders, J., Beiler, R., & Markol, C.A. (Eds.). (2014). *Writing with style: Formatting for fun* [Monograph]. Retrieved from http://www.onlinedatabaseurl.edu/limitedcirculation

Non-English Reference Book Translated into English, Entire Book, No Author, with Three Editors

Seja Feliz. (2014). In R. Guerrimo, R. Rodriguez, & S. Lorenzo (Eds.), *Bondade E' A Resposta* [Goodness is the answer] (13th ed.). Mexico City, Mexico: Anchor Press.

Multivolume Work with Three Editors, No Author

Anders, J., Beiler, R., & Markol, C.A. (Eds.). (2014). *Encyclopedia of Accounting Terms* (Vols. 1-8). Dacono, CO: Anchor Press.

Multivolume Work with Three Editors, No Author, Other than First Edition

Anders, J., Beiler, R., & Markol, C.A. (Eds.). (2014). *Encyclopedia of Accounting Terms* (3rd ed., Vols. 1-8). Dacono, CO: Anchor Press.

Multivolume Work with Three Editors, Other than First Edition, Online

Anders, J., Beiler, R., & Markol, C.A. (Eds.). (2014). *Encyclopedia of Accounting Terms* (3rd ed., Vols. 1-8). Retrieved from http://www.youversustheworld.com/encyclopedia

Three Editors, No Author, Chapter in Book

We format for fun. (2014). In R. Miller, P. M. Warfield, & R. Marcot (Eds.), *Writing with style* (pp. 91-103). New York, NY: Anchor Press.

Three Editors, No Author, Electronic Book/Ebook

Anders, J., Beiler, R., & Markol, C.A. (Eds.). (2014). *Writing with style.* Retrieved from http://www.youversustheworld.com/ebookreferences

Three Editors, No Author, Electronic Version of Print Version (Kindle, Nook, etc.)

Anders, J., Beiler, R., & Markol, C.A. (Eds.). (2014). *APA made easy* [Kindle DX version]. Retrieved from http://www.youversustheworld.com

Three Editors, No Author, Chapter in Electronic Book/Ebook

We format for fun. (2014). In R. Miller, P. M. Warfield, & R. Marcot (Eds.), *Writing with style* (pp. 91-103). Retrieved from http://www.youversustheworld/bookchapter

Three Editors, No Author, Chapter in Electronic Book/Ebook, with DOI

We format for fun. (2014). In R. Miller, P. M. Warfield, & R. Marcot (Eds.), *Writing with style* (pp. 91-103). doi:10.1234567890

Reference Book with Three Editors, No Author

Anders, J., Beiler, R., & Markol, C.A. (Eds.). (2014). *References in obscurity*. Wauconda, IL: Anchor Press.

Entry in Reference Book with Three Editors, No Author

References in obscurity. (2014). In R. Miller, P. M. Warfield, & R. Marcot (Eds.), *Getting references right* (3rd ed., Vol. 8). Wauconda, IL: Anchor Press.

Entry in Online Reference Book with Three Editors, No Author

References in obscurity. (2014). In R. Miller, P. M. Warfield, & R. Marcot (Eds.), *Getting references right* (3rd ed., Vol. 8). Retrieved from http://www.youversustheworld.com/referencesbooks

Entry in Online Reference Book with Three Editors, No Author, with DOI

References in obscurity. (2014). In R. Miller, P. M. Warfield, & R. Marcot (Eds.), *Getting references right* (3rd ed., Vol. 8). doi:10.1234567890

Entry in Online Reference Book with Three Editors, No Author, Alternative Edition Example

References in obscurity. (2014). In R. Miller, P. M. Warfield, & R. Marcot (Eds.), *Getting references right* (Spring 2008 ed.). Retrieved from http://www.youversustheworld.com/referencesbooks

Edited Books with One Author

A Quick Overview : **Edited Books with One Author**

Sample Reference Structure:

Author Last Name, First Initials. (Date of Publication). Title of chapter. In Editor First Initial. Last Name (Ed.), *Title of book* (page number). City, State Initials: Publisher.

Example:

Anders, J. (2012). Headings in APA. In S. Johnson (Ed.), *APA made easy* (pp. 95-97). New York, NY: Anchor Press.

Electronic Sample

Author Last Name, First Initials. (Date of Publication). Title of Chapter. In Editor First Initial. Last Name (Ed.), *Title of book* (page number). Retrieved from http://nameofurl.com

Electronic Example

Anders, J. C. (2014). Headings in APA. In S. Johnson (Ed.), *APA made easy*. Retrieved from http://www.youversustheworld.com/editedebooks

Sample In-Text Citations

Example #1: Paraphrase

According to a book edited by Anders (2012), writing in APA format can be easy.

Example #2: Paraphrase

With so many resources available, writing in APA format can be easy (Anders, 2012).

Example #3: Direct Quote

Anders (2012) stated, "Writing in APA format can be easy" (p. 8).

Example #4: Direct Quote

"Writing in APA format can be easy" (Anders, 2012, p. 8).

Edited Books with One Author

Edited Book with One Author, Standard Date

Anders, J. (2012). Headings in APA. In S. Johnson (Ed.), *APA made easy* (pp. 95-97). New York, NY: Anchor Press.

Edited Book with One Author, No Date

Anders, J. (n.d.). Headings in APA. In S. Johnson (Ed.), *APA made easy* (pp. 95-97). New York, NY: Anchor Press.

Edited Book with One Author, Republished Date - Use latest date listed

Anders, J. (2012). In S. Johnson (Ed.). *APA made easy* (p. 95). New York, NY: Anchor Press.

In Text Citation Example - Cite both the original published date and the date of the republished version:
(Anders, 2000/2014).

Edited Book with One Author, Edition Other Than First

Anders, J. (2012). Headings in APA. In S. Johnson (Ed.), *APA made easy* (3rd ed., pp. 95-97). New York, NY: Anchor Press.

Edited Book with One Author, Series Editor

Anders, J. (2012). Headings in APA. In S. Johnson (Series Ed.), *APA made easy* (pp. 95-97). New York, NY: Anchor Press.

Edited Book with One Author, Revised Edition

Anders, J. (2012). Headings in APA. In S. Johnson (Ed.), *APA made easy* (Rev. ed., pp. 95-97). New York, NY: Anchor Press.

Edited Book with One Author, Title with Subtitle

Anders, J. (2012). Headings in APA. In S. Johnson (Ed.), *APA made easy: An important step in formatting* (pp. 95-97). New York, NY: Anchor Press.

Edited Book with One Author, No Date, Title with Subtitle

Anders, J. (n.d.). Headings in APA. In S. Johnson (Ed.), *APA made easy: An important step in formatting* (pp. 95-97). New York, NY: Anchor Press.

Edited Book with One Author, Title with Proper Noun

Anders, J. R. (2014). In S. Johnson (Ed.). *The life and times of J. Edgar Hoover* (pp. 103-105). New York, NY: Anchor Press.

Edited Book with One Author, Hyphenated Name

Anders, J. -A. (2012). Headings in APA. In S. Johnson (Ed.), *APA made easy* (pp. 95-97). New York, NY: Anchor Press.

Edited Book with One Author, Title with Subtitle, Edition Other Than First

Anders, J. (2012). Headings in APA. In S. Johnson (Ed.), *APA made easy: An important step in formatting* (3rd ed., pp. 95-97). New York, NY: Anchor Press.

Edited Book with One Author, Title with Series Name

Anders, J. (2012). Headings in APA. In S. Johnson (Ed.), *APA made easy: Vol. 4. An important step in formatting* (pp. 95-97). New York, NY: Anchor Press.

Edited Book with One Author, Limited Circulation Book, Not Online

Anders, J. A. (2014). Creating a new metaphor. In S. Johnson (Ed.), *Writing with style: Formatting for fun.* (Available from Baker, 122 South Salem Street, Billings, MT, 59101)

Edited Book with One Author, Limited Circulation, From Online Database

Anders, J. A. (2014). Creating a new metaphor. In S. Johnson (Ed.), *Writing with style: Formatting for fun.* Retrieved from http://www.onlinedatabaseurl.edu/limitedcirculation

Edited Book with One Author, Monograph

Anders, J. A. (2014). Creating a new metaphor. In S. Johnson (Ed.). *Writing with style: Formatting for fun* [Monograph]. Retrieved from http://www.onlinedatabaseurl.edu/limitedcirculation

Chapter in Edited Book with One Author

Anders, J. A. (2014). Creating a new metaphor. In R. Miller (Ed.). *Writing with style* (pp. 93-103). New York, NY: Anchor Press.

Chapter in Edited Book with One Author, Republished Date - Use latest date listed

Anders, J. (2012). In S. Johnson (Ed.). *APA made easy* (p. 95). New York, NY: Anchor Press.

Chapter in Edited Book with One Author, Edition Other Than First

Anders, J. (2012). Headings in APA. In S. Johnson (Ed.), *APA made easy* (3rd ed., pp. 95-97). New York, NY: Anchor Press.

Chapter in Edited Book with One Author, Revised Edition

Anders, J. (2012). Headings in APA. In S. Johnson (Ed.), *APA made easy* (Rev. ed., pp. 95-97). New York, NY: Anchor Press.

Chapter in Edited Book with One Author, Title with Subtitle

Anders, J. (2012). Headings in APA. In S. Johnson (Ed.), *APA made easy: An important step in formatting* (pp. 95-97). New York, NY: Anchor Press.

Chapter in Edited Book with One Author, No Date, Title with Subtitle

Anders, J. (n.d.). Headings in APA. In S. Johnson (Ed.), *APA made easy: An important step in formatting* (pp. 95-97). New York, NY: Anchor Press.

Chapter in Edited Book with One Author, Title with Proper Noun

Anders, J. R. (2014). In S. Johnson (Ed.). *The life and times of J. Edgar Hoover* (pp. 103-105). New York, NY: Anchor Press.

Chapter in Edited Book with One Author, Hyphenated Name

Anders, J. -A. (2012). Headings in APA. In S. Johnson (Ed.), *APA made easy* (pp. 95-97). New York, NY: Anchor Press.

Chapter in Edited Book with One Author, Title with Subtitle, Edition Other Than First

Anders, J. (2012). Headings in APA. In S. Johnson (Ed.), *APA made easy: An important step in formatting* (3rd ed., pp. 95-97). New York, NY: Anchor Press.

Chapter in Edited Book with One Author, Title with Series Name

Anders, J. (2012). Headings in APA. In S. Johnson (Ed.), *APA made easy: Vol. 4. An important step in formatting* (pp. 95-97). New York, NY: Anchor Press.

Chapter in Edited Book, English Translation, One Author

Anders, J. R. (2014). Creating a new metaphor (R. Miller, Trans.). In B. Reynolds (Ed.), *Formatting for dummies* (pp. 3-56). Dallas, TX: Anchor Press.

Chapter in Edited Book, English Translation, One Author, Reprinted from Another Source

Anders, J. R. (2014). Creating a new metaphor (R. Miller, Trans.). In B. Reynolds (Ed.), *Formatting for dummies* (pp. 3-56). Dallas, TX: Anchor Press. (Reprinted from *Formatting for fun*, pp. 78-121, by B. B. Newby, Ed., 2000, Billings, MT: Newport Press)

Chapter in Edited Book with One Author, Limited Circulation Book, Not Online

Anders, J. A. (2014). Creating a new metaphor. In S. Johnson (Ed.), *Writing with style: Formatting for fun.* (Available from Baker, 122 South Salem Street, Billings, MT, 59101)

Chapter in Edited Book with One Author, Limited Circulation, From Online Database

Anders, J. A. (2014). Creating a new metaphor. In S. Johnson (Ed.), *Writing with style: Formatting for fun.* New York, NY: Anchor Press.

Chapter in Edited Book with One Author, Monograph

Anders, J. A. (2014). Creating a new metaphor. In S. Johnson (Ed.). *Writing with style: Formatting for fun* [Monograph]. New York, NY: Anchor Press.

Edited Book with One Author, Electronic Version/Ebook

Anders, J. C. (2014). Headings in APA. In S. Johnson (Ed.), *APA made easy.* Retrieved from http://www.youversustheworld.com/editedebooks

Edited Book with One Author, Electronic Version/Ebook, with DOI

Anders, J. C. (2014). Headings in APA. In S. Johnson (Ed.), *APA made easy.* doi: 10.1234567890

Edited Book with One Author, Electronic Version of Print Version

Anders, J. C. (2014). Headings in APA. In S. Johnson (Ed.), *APA made easy* [Kindle DX version] (pp. 95-97). Retrieved from http://www.apamadeeasy.com/editedbooks

Edited Book with One Author, Electronic Version of Republished Print Book

Anders, J. C. (2014). Headings in APA. In S. Johnson (Ed.), *APA made easy*. Retrieved from http://www.youversustheworld.com/electronic/republishedurl

Edited Book with One Author, Electronic Version/Ebook, Edition Other Than First

Anders, J. (2012). Headings in APA. In S. Johnson (Ed.), *APA made easy* (3rd ed., pp. 95-97). Retrieved from http://www.youversustheworld.com/editedebooks

Edited Book with One Author, Electronic Version/Ebook, Series Editor

Anders, J. (2012). Headings in APA. In S. Johnson (Series Ed.), *APA made easy* (pp. 95-97). Retrieved from http://www.youversustheworld.com/editedebooks

Edited Book with One Author, Electronic Version/Ebook, Revised Edition

Anders, J. (2012). Headings in APA. In S. Johnson (Ed.), *APA made easy* (Rev. ed., pp. 95-97). Retrieved from http://www.youversustheworld.com/editedebooks

Edited Book with One Author, Electronic Version/Ebook, Title with Subtitle

Anders, J. (2012). Headings in APA. In S. Johnson (Ed.), *APA made easy: An important step in formatting* (pp. 95-97). Retrieved from http://www.youversustheworld.com/editedebooks

Edited Book with One Author, Electronic Version/Ebook, No Date, Title with Subtitle

Anders, J. (n.d.). Headings in APA. In S. Johnson (Ed.), *APA made easy: An important step in formatting* (pp. 95-97). Retrieved from http://www.youversustheworld.com/editedebooks

Edited Book with One Author, Electronic Version/Ebook, No Date, Title with Subtitle, with DOI

Anders, J. (n.d.). Headings in APA. In S. Johnson (Ed.), *APA made easy: An important step in formatting* (pp. 95-97). doi:10:1234567890

Edited Book with One Author, Electronic Version/Ebook, Title with Proper Noun

Anders, J. R. (2014). In S. Johnson (Ed.). *The life and times of J. Edgar Hoover* (pp. 103-105). Retrieved from http://www.youversustheworld.com/editedebooks

Edited Book with One Author, Electronic Version/Ebook, Hyphenated Name

Anders, J. -A. (2012). Headings in APA. In S. Johnson (Ed.), *APA made easy* (pp. 95-97). Retrieved from http://www.youversustheworld.com/editedebooks

Edited Book with One Author, Electronic Version/Ebook, Title with Subtitle, Edition Other Than First

Anders, J. (2012). Headings in APA. In S. Johnson (Ed.), *APA made easy: An important step in formatting* (3rd ed., pp. 95-97). Retrieved from http://www.youversustheworld.com/editedebooks

Edited Book with One Author, Electronic Version/Ebook, Title with Series Name

Anders, J. (2012). Headings in APA. In S. Johnson (Ed.), *APA made easy: Vol. 4. An important step in formatting* (pp. 95-97). Retrieved from http://www.youversustheworld.com/editedebooks

Edited Book with One Author, Electronic Version/Ebook, Title with Series Name, with DOI

Anders, J. (2012). Headings in APA. In S. Johnson (Ed.), *APA made easy: Vol. 4. An important step in formatting* (pp. 95-97). doi:10.1234567890

Chapter of Edited Electronic Book/Ebook with One Author

Anders, J. A. (2014). Creating a new metaphor. In R. Miller (Ed.). *Writing with style* (pp. 93-103). Retrieved from http://www.youversustheworld.com/ebookchapterreferences

Chapter of Edited Electronic Book/Ebook with One Author, with DOI

Anders, J. A. (2014). Creating a new metaphor. In R. Miller (Ed.). *Writing with style* (pp. 93-103). doi:10.1234567890

Chapter in Edited Electronic Book/Ebook of Print Version with One Author

Anders, J. (2014). Creating a new metaphor. In R. McClure (Ed.). *Writing with style* [iBooks version]. Retrieved from http://www.ibooks.com/chapterreferences

Chapter in Edited Electronic Book/Ebook of Print Version with One Author, with DOI

Anders, J. (2014). Creating a new metaphor. In R. McClure (Ed.). *Writing with style* [iBooks version]. doi:10.1234567890

Chapter in Edited Electronic Book/Ebook of Print Version from Republished Book with One Author

Anders, J. (2014). Creating a new metaphor. In R. McClure (Ed.). *Writing with style* (Vol. 1, pp. 105-144). Retrieved from http://www.youversustheworld.com/chapterreference

Edited Reference Book with One Author - Only list Editor's Name

Anders, J. (Ed.). (2014). *References in obscurity*. Wauconda, IL: Anchor Press.

Entry in Reference Book with One Editor, One Author

Anders, J. (2014). References in obscurity. In R. Miller (Ed.), *Getting references right* (3rd ed., Vol. 8). Wauconda, IL: Anchor Press.

Entry in Online Reference Book with One Editor, One Author

Anders, J. (2014). References in obscurity. In R. Miller (Ed.), *Getting references right* (3rd ed., Vol. 8). Retrieved from http://www.youversustheworld.com/referencesbooks

Entry in Online Reference Book with One Editor, One Author, with DOI

Anders, J. (2014). References in obscurity. In R. Miller (Ed.), *Getting references right* (3rd ed., Vol. 8). doi:10.1234567890

Entry in Online Reference Book with One Editor, One Author, Alternative Edition Example

Anders, J. (2014). References in obscurity. In R. Miller (Ed.), *Getting references right* (Spring 2008 ed.). Retrieved from http://www.youversustheworld.com/referencesbooks

Edited Books with Two Authors

A Quick Overview : **Edited Books with Two Authors**

Sample Reference Structure:

Author Last Name, First Initials. & Second Author Last Name, First Initial. (Date of Publication). Title of Chapter. In Editor First Initial. Last Name (Ed.), *Title of book* (page number). City, State Initials: Publisher.

Example:

Anders, J. (2012). Headings in APA. In S. Johnson (Ed.), *APA made easy* (pp. 95-97). New York, NY: Anchor Press.

Electronic Sample

Author Last Name, First Initials. & Second Author Last Name, First Initial. (Date of Publication). Title of Chapter. In Editor First Initial. Last Name (Ed.), *Title of book* (page number). Retrieved from http://nameofurl.com

Electronic Example

Anders, J., & Beiler, R. (2012). Headings in APA. In S. Johnson (Ed.), *APA made easy*. Retrieved from http://www.youversustheworld.com/editedebooks

Sample In-Text Citations

Example #1: Paraphrase

According to a book edited by Anders and Beiler's (2012), writing in APA format can be easy.

Example #2: Paraphrase

With so many resources available, writing in APA format can be easy (Anders & Beiler, 2012).

Example #3: Direct Quote

Anders and Beiler (2012) stated, "Writing in APA format can be easy" (p. 8).

Example #2: Direct Quote

With so many resources available, writing in APA format can be easy (Anders & Beiler, 2012, p. 8).

Edited Books with Two Authors

Edited Book with Two Authors, Standard Date

Anders, J., & Beiler, R. (2012). Headings in APA. In S. Johnson (Ed.), *APA made easy* (pp. 95-97). New York, NY: Anchor Press.

Edited Book with Two Authors, No Date

Anders, J., & Beiler, R. (n.d.). Headings in APA. In S. Johnson (Ed.), *APA made easy* (pp. 95-97). New York, NY: Anchor Press.

Edited Book with Two Authors, Republished Date - Use latest date listed

Anders, J., & Beiler, R. (2012). In S. Johnson (Ed.). *APA made easy* (p. 95). New York, NY: Anchor Press.

In Text Citation Example - Cite both the original published date and the date of the republished version:
(Anders & Beiler, 2000/2014).

Edited Book with Two Authors, Edition Other Than First

Anders, J., & Beiler, R. (2012). Headings in APA. In S. Johnson (Ed.), *APA made easy* (3rd ed., pp. 95-97). New York, NY: Anchor Press.

Edited Book with Two Authors, Series Editor

Anders, J., & Beiler, R. (2012). Headings in APA. In S. Johnson (Series Ed.), *APA made easy* (pp. 95-97). New York, NY: Anchor Press.

Edited Book with Two Authors, Revised Edition

Anders, J., & Beiler, R. (2012). Headings in APA. In S. Johnson (Ed.), *APA made easy* (Rev. ed., pp. 95-97). New York, NY: Anchor Press.

Edited Book with Two Authors, Title with Subtitle

Anders, J., & Beiler, R. (2012). Headings in APA. In S. Johnson (Ed.), *APA made easy: An important step in formatting* (pp. 95-97). New York, NY: Anchor Press.

Edited Book with Two Authors, No Date, Title with Subtitle

Anders, J., & Beiler, R. (n.d.). Headings in APA. In S. Johnson (Ed.), *APA made easy: An important step in formatting* (pp. 95-97). New York, NY: Anchor Press.

Edited Book with Two Authors, Title with Proper Noun

Anders, J., & Beiler, R. (2014). In S. Johnson (Ed.). *The life and times of J. Edgar Hoover* (pp. 103-105). New York, NY: Anchor Press.

Edited Book with Two Authors, Hyphenated Name

Anders, J. -A., & Beiler, R. (2012). Headings in APA. In S. Johnson (Ed.), *APA made easy* (pp. 95-97). New York, NY: Anchor Press.

Edited Book with Two Authors, Title with Subtitle, Edition Other Than First

Anders, J., & Beiler, R. (2012). Headings in APA. In S. Johnson (Ed.), *APA made easy: An important step in formatting* (3rd ed., pp. 95-97). New York, NY: Anchor Press.

Edited Book with Two Authors, Title with Series Name

Anders, J., & Beiler, R. (2012). Headings in APA. In S. Johnson (Ed.), *APA made easy: Vol. 4. An important step in formatting* (pp. 95-97). New York, NY: Anchor Press.

Edited Book with Two Authors, Limited Circulation Book, Not Online

Anders, J., & Beiler, R. (2014). Creating a new metaphor. In S. Johnson (Ed.), *Writing with style: Formatting for fun.* (Available from Baker, 122 South Salem Street, Billings, MT, 59101)

Edited Book with Two Authors, Limited Circulation, From Online Database

Anders, J., & Beiler, R. (2014). Creating a new metaphor. In S. Johnson (Ed.), *Writing with style: Formatting for fun.* Retrieved from http://www.onlinedatabaseurl.edu/limitedcirculation

Edited Book with Two Authors, Monograph

Anders, J., & Beiler, R. (2014). Creating a new metaphor. In S. Johnson (Ed.). *Writing with style: Formatting for fun* [Monograph]. Retrieved from http://www.onlinedatabaseurl.edu/limitedcirculation

Chapter in Edited Book with Two Authors

Anders, J., & Beiler, R. (2014). Creating a new metaphor. In R. Miller (Ed.). *Writing with style* (pp. 93-103). New York, NY: Anchor Press.

Chapter in Edited Book with Two Authors, Republished Date - Use latest date listed

Anders, J., & Beiler, R. (2012). In S. Johnson (Ed.). *APA made easy* (p. 95). New York, NY: Anchor Press.

Chapter in Edited Book with Two Authors, Edition Other Than First

Anders, J., & Beiler, R. (2012). Headings in APA. In S. Johnson (Ed.), *APA made easy* (3rd ed., pp. 95-97). New York, NY: Anchor Press.

Chapter in Edited Book with Two Authors, Revised Edition

Anders, J., & Beiler, R. (2012). Headings in APA. In S. Johnson (Ed.), *APA made easy* (Rev. ed., pp. 95-97). New York, NY: Anchor Press.

Chapter in Edited Book with Two Authors, Title with Subtitle

Anders, J., & Beiler, R. (2012). Headings in APA. In S. Johnson (Ed.), *APA made easy: An important step in formatting* (pp. 95-97). New York, NY: Anchor Press.

Chapter in Edited Book with Two Authors, No Date, Title with Subtitle

Anders, J., & Beiler, R. (n.d.). Headings in APA. In S. Johnson (Ed.), *APA made easy: An important step in formatting* (pp. 95-97). New York, NY: Anchor Press.

Chapter in Edited Book with Two Authors, Title with Proper Noun

Anders, J., & Beiler, R. (2014). In S. Johnson (Ed.). *The life and times of J. Edgar Hoover* (pp. 103-105). New York, NY: Anchor Press.

Chapter in Edited Book with Two Authors, Hyphenated Name

Anders, J. -A., & Beiler, R. (2012). Headings in APA. In S. Johnson (Ed.), *APA made easy* (pp. 95-97). New York, NY: Anchor Press.

Chapter in Edited Book with Two Authors, Title with Subtitle, Edition Other Than First

Anders, J., & Beiler, R. (2012). Headings in APA. In S. Johnson (Ed.), *APA made easy: An important step in formatting* (3rd ed., pp. 95-97). New York, NY: Anchor Press.

Chapter in Edited Book with Two Authors, Title with Series Name

Anders, J., & Beiler, R. (2012). Headings in APA. In S. Johnson (Ed.), *APA made easy: Vol. 4. An important step in formatting* (pp. 95-97). New York, NY: Anchor Press.

Chapter in Edited Book, English Translation, Two Authors

Anders, J., & Beiler, R. (2014). Creating a new metaphor (R. Miller, Trans.). In B. Reynolds (Ed.), *Formatting for dummies* (pp. 3-56). Dallas, TX: Anchor Press.

Chapter in Edited Book, English Translation, Two Authors, Reprinted from Another Source

Anders, J., & Beiler, R. (2012). Creating a new metaphor (R. Miller, Trans.). In B. Reynolds (Ed.), *Formatting for dummies* (pp. 3-56). Dallas, TX: Anchor Press. (Reprinted from *Formatting for fun*, pp. 78-121, by B. B. Newby, Ed., 2000, Billings, MT: Newport Press)

Chapter in Edited Book with Two Authors, Limited Circulation Book, Not Online

Anders, J., & Beiler, R. (2012). Creating a new metaphor. In S. Johnson (Ed.), *Writing with style: Formatting for fun.* (Available from Baker, 122 South Salem Street, Billings, MT, 59101)

Chapter in Edited Book with Two Authors, Limited Circulation, From Online Database

Anders, J., & Beiler, R. (2012). Creating a new metaphor. In S. Johnson (Ed.), *Writing with style: Formatting for fun.* New York, NY: Anchor Press.

Chapter in Edited Book with Two Authors, Monograph

Anders, J., & Beiler, R. (2012). Creating a new metaphor. In S. Johnson (Ed.). *Writing with style: Formatting for fun* [Monograph]. New York, NY: Anchor Press.

Edited Book with Two Authors, Electronic Version/Ebook

Anders, J., & Beiler, R. (2012). Headings in APA. In S. Johnson (Ed.), *APA made easy*. Retrieved from http://www.youversustheworld.com/editedebooks

Edited Book with Two Authors, Electronic Version/Ebook, with DOI

Anders, J., & Beiler, R. (2012). Headings in APA. In S. Johnson (Ed.), *APA made easy*. doi: 10.1234567890

Edited Book with Two Authors, Electronic Version of Print Version

Anders, J., & Beiler, R. (2012). Headings in APA. In S. Johnson (Ed.), *APA made easy* [Kindle DX version] (pp. 95-97). Retrieved from http://www.apamadeeasy.com/editedbooks

Edited Book with Two Authors, Electronic Version of Republished Print Book

Anders, J., & Beiler, R. (2012). Headings in APA. In S. Johnson (Ed.), *APA made easy*. Retrieved from http://www.youversustheworld.com/electronic/republishedurl

Edited Book with Two Authors, Electronic Version/Ebook, Edition Other Than First

Anders, J., & Beiler, R. (2012). Headings in APA. In S. Johnson (Ed.), *APA made easy* (3rd ed., pp. 95-97). Retrieved from http://www.youversustheworld.com/editedebooks

Edited Book with Two Authors, Electronic Version/Ebook, Series Editor

Anders, J., & Beiler, R. (2012). Headings in APA. In S. Johnson (Series Ed.), *APA made easy* (pp. 95-97). Retrieved from http://www.youversustheworld.com/editedebooks

Edited Book with Two Authors, Electronic Version/Ebook, Revised Edition

Anders, J., & Beiler, R. (2012). Headings in APA. In S. Johnson (Ed.), *APA made easy* (Rev. ed., pp. 95-97). Retrieved from http://www.youversustheworld.com/editedebooks

Edited Book with Two Authors, Electronic Version/Ebook, Title with Subtitle

Anders, J., & Beiler, R. (2012). Headings in APA. In S. Johnson (Ed.), *APA made easy: An important step in formatting* (pp. 95-97). Retrieved from http://www.youversustheworld.com/editedebooks

Edited Book with Two Authors, Electronic Version/Ebook, No Date, Title with Subtitle

Anders, J., & Beiler, R. (n.d.). Headings in APA. In S. Johnson (Ed.), *APA made easy: An important step in formatting* (pp. 95-97). Retrieved from http://www.youversustheworld.com/editedebooks

Edited Book with Two Authors, Electronic Version/Ebook, No Date, Title with Subtitle, with DOI

Anders, J., & Beiler, R. (n.d.). Headings in APA. In S. Johnson (Ed.), *APA made easy: An important step in formatting* (pp. 95-97). doi:10:1234567890

Edited Book with Two Authors, Electronic Version/Ebook, Title with Proper Noun

Anders, J., & Beiler, R. (2014). In S. Johnson (Ed.). *The life and times of J. Edgar Hoover* (pp. 103-105). Retrieved from http://www.youversustheworld.com/editedebooks

Edited Book with Two Authors, Electronic Version/Ebook, Hyphenated Name

Anders, J. -A., & Beiler, R. (2012). Headings in APA. In S. Johnson (Ed.), *APA made easy* (pp. 95-97). Retrieved from http://www.youversustheworld.com/editedebooks

Edited Book with Two Authors, Electronic Version/Ebook, Title with Subtitle, Edition Other Than First

Anders, J., & Beiler, R. (2012). Headings in APA. In S. Johnson (Ed.), *APA made easy: An important step in formatting* (3rd ed., pp. 95-97). Retrieved from http://www.youversustheworld.com/editedebooks

Edited Book with Two Authors, Electronic Version/Ebook, Title with Series Name

Anders, J., & Beiler, R. (2012). Headings in APA. In S. Johnson (Ed.), *APA made easy: Vol. 4. An important step in formatting* (pp. 95-97). Retrieved from http://www.youversustheworld.com/editedebooks

Edited Book with Two Authors, Electronic Version/Ebook, Title with Series Name, with DOI

Anders, J., & Beiler, R. (2012). Headings in APA. In S. Johnson (Ed.), *APA made easy: Vol. 4. An important step in formatting* (pp. 95-97). doi:10.1234567890

Chapter of Edited Electronic Book/Ebook with Two Authors

Anders, J., & Beiler, R. (2014). Creating a new metaphor. In R. Miller (Ed.). *Writing with style* (pp. 93-103). Retrieved from http://www.youversustheworld.com/ebookchapterreferences

Chapter of Edited Electronic Book/Ebook with Two Authors, with DOI

Anders, J., & Beiler, R. (2014). Creating a new metaphor. In R. Miller (Ed.). *Writing with style* (pp. 93-103). doi:10.1234567890

Chapter in Edited Electronic Book/Ebook of Print Version with Two Authors

Anders, J., & Beiler, R. (2014). Creating a new metaphor. In R. McClure (Ed.). *Writing with style* [iBooks version]. Retrieved from http://www.ibooks.com/chapterreferences

Chapter in Edited Electronic Book/Ebook of Print Version with Two Authors, with DOI

Anders, J., & Beiler, R. (2014). Creating a new metaphor. In R. McClure (Ed.). *Writing with style* [iBooks version]. doi:10.1234567890

Chapter in Edited Electronic Book/Ebook of Print Version from Republished Book with Two Authors

Anders, J., & Beiler, R. (2014). Creating a new metaphor. In R. McClure (Ed.). *Writing with style* (Vol. 1, pp. 105-144). Retrieved from http://www.youversustheworld.com/chapterreference

Edited Reference Book with Two Authors - Only list Editor's Name

Anders, J., & Beiler, R. (Ed.). (2014). *References in obscurity*. Wauconda, IL: Anchor Press.

Entry in Reference Book with Two Editors, Two Authors

Anders, J., & Beiler, R. (2014). References in obscurity. In R. Miller, & D. Zen (Eds.), *Getting references right* (3rd ed., Vol. 8). Wauconda, IL: Anchor Press.

Entry in Online Reference Book with Two Editors, Two Authors

Anders, J., & Beiler, R. (2014). References in obscurity. In R. Miller, & D. Zen (Eds.), *Getting references right* (3rd ed., Vol. 8). Retrieved from http://www.youversustheworld.com/referencesbooks

Entry in Online Reference Book with Two Editors, Two Authors, with DOI

Anders, J., & Beiler, R. (2014). References in obscurity. In R. Miller, & D. Zen (Eds.), *Getting references right* (3rd ed., Vol. 8). doi:10.1234567890

Entry in Online Reference Book with Two Editors, Two Authors, Alternative Edition Example

Anders, J., & Beiler, R. (2014). References in obscurity. In R. Miller, & D. Zen (Eds.), *Getting references right* (Spring 2008 ed.). Retrieved from http://www.youversustheworld.com/referencesbooks

Books with One Author

A Quick Overview : **Books with One Author**

Sample Reference Structure:

Author Last Name, First Initial. (Year of Publication). *Title of publication.* City, State Initials of Publication: Publisher.

Example:

Anders, J. (2012). *APA made easy.* New York, NY: Anchor Press.

Electronic Sample

Author Last Name, First Initial. (Year of Publication). *Title of publication.* City, State Initials of Publication: Publisher. Retrieved from http://nameofurl.com

Electronic Example

Anders, J. (2012). *APA made easy.* New York, NY: Anchor Press. Retrieved from http://www.youversustheworld.com/editedebooks

Sample In-Text Citations

Example #1: Paraphrase
According to Anders (2012), writing in APA format can be easy.

Example #2: Paraphrase
With so many resources available, writing in APA format can be easy (Anders, 2012).

Example #3: Direct Quote
Anders (2012) stated, "Writing in APA format can be easy" (p. iv).

Example #4: Direct Quote
With so many resources available, writing in APA format can be easy (Anders, 2012, p. 19).

Books with One Author

Book with One Author, Standard Date of Publication

Anders, J. (2012). *APA made easy*. New York, NY: Anchor Press.

Book with One Author, No Date

Anders, J. (n.d.). *APA made easy*. New York, NY: Anchor Press.

Book with One Author, Republished Date - Use the latest date listed

Anders, J. (2012). *APA made easy*. New York, NY: Anchor Press.

In Text Citation Example - Cite both the original published date and the date of the republished version:

(Anders, 2000/2014).

Book with One Author, Edition Other Than First

Anders, J. (2012). *APA made easy* (4th ed.). New York, NY: Anchor Press.

Book with One Author, Revised Edition

Anders, J. (2012). *APA made easy* (Rev. ed.). New York, NY: Anchor Press.

Book with One Author, Title with Subtitle

Anders, J. (2012). *APA made easy: Writing with style*. New York, NY: Anchor Press.

Book with One Author, No Date, Title with Subtitle

Anders, J. (n.d.). *APA made easy: Writing with style*. New York, NY: Anchor Press.

Book with One Author, Title with Proper Noun

Anders, J. (2014). *The life and times of J. Edgar Hoover*. New York, NY: Anchor Press.

Book with One Author with Hyphenated Name

Anders, J. -R. (2014). *The life and times of J. Edgar Hoover*. New York, NY: Anchor Press.

Book with One Author, Title with Subtitle, Edition Other than First

Anders, J. (2014). *APA made easy: Writing with style* (4th ed.). New York, NY: Anchor Press.

Book with One Author, No Date, Title with Subtitle, Edition Other than First

Anders, J. (n.d.). *APA made easy: Writing with style* (4th ed.). New York, NY: Anchor Press.

Book with One Author, Title with Series

Anders, J. (2012). *APA made easy: Vol. 4. Writing with style.* New York, NY: Anchor Press.

Book with One Author, Limited Circulation, Not Online

Anders, J. A. (2014). *Creating a new metaphor.* (Available from Baker, 122 South Salem Street, Billings, MT. 59101)

Book with One Author, Limited Circulation, From Database

Anders, J. A. (2014). *Creating a new metaphor.* Retrieved from http://www.nameofonlinedatabaseurl.edu/onlinelimitedcirculation

Book with One Author, Monograph

Anders, J. A. (2014). *Creating a new metaphor* [Monograph]. Retrieved from http://www.nameofonlinedatabaseurl.edu/onlinelimitedcirculation

Book with One Author, No Date, Monograph

Anders, J. A. (n.d.). *Creating a new metaphor* [Monograph]. Retrieved from http://www.namcofonlinedatabaseurl.edu/onlinelimitedcirculation

Book with One Corporate Author

American Psychological Association. (2014). *APA writing and formatting.* Washington, DC: Anchor Press.

In Text Citation Example:

The American Psychological Associate (APA, 2014) states …

Alternatively,

leading to greater affluence among this population (American Psychological Association [APA], 2014).

After the first in text citation, you may abbreviate the name of the group so long as it is discernable to the reader which group you are referring to. Thus:

The APA (2014) states …
Leading to greater affluence among this population (APA, 2014).

Chapter in Book with One Author

Anders, J. A. (2014). Writing in style. In R. Miller (Ed.), *Writing Fundamentals* (pp. 93-103). New York, NY: Anchor Press.

Chapter in Book with One Author, Republished Date - Use the latest date listed

Anders, J. (2012). Writing in style. In R. Miller (Ed.), *APA made easy*. New York, NY: Anchor Press.

Chapter in Book with One Author, Title with Subtitle

Anders, J. (2012). Writing in style. In R. Miller (Ed.), *APA made easy: A new way of formatting*. New York, NY: Anchor Press.

Chapter in Book, English Translation, One Author

Anders, J. R. (2014). Creating a new metaphor (R. Miller, Trans.). In B. Reynolds (Ed.), *Formatting for dummies* (pp. 3-56). Dallas, TX: Anchor Press.

Chapter in Book with One Author, Title with Proper Noun

Anders, J. (2014). Writing in style. In R. Miller (Ed.), *The life and times of J. Edgar Hoover*. New York, NY: Anchor Press.

Chapter in Book with One Author, Limited Circulation, Not Online

Anders, J. A. (2014). Writing in style. In R. Miller (Ed.), *Creating a new metaphor*. (Available from Baker, 122 South Salem Street, Billings, MT. 59101)

Chapter in Book with One Author, Limited Circulation, From Database - include URL of database where chapter can be found

Anders, J. A. (2014). Writing in style. In R. Miller (Ed.), *Creating a new metaphor*. Retrieved from http://www.nameofonlinedatabaseurl.edu/onlinelimitedcirculation

Chapter in Book, English Translation, One Author

Anders, J. R. (2014). Creating a new metaphor (R. Miller, Trans.). In B. Reynolds (Ed.), *Formatting for dummies* (pp. 3-56). Dallas, TX: Anchor Press.

Chapter in Book, English Translation, One Author, Reprinted from Another Source

Anders, J. R. (2014). Creating a new metaphor (R. Miller, Trans.). In B. Reynolds (Ed.), *Formatting for dummies* (pp. 3-56). Dallas, TX: Anchor Press. (Reprinted from *Formatting for fun*, pp. 78-121, by B. B. Newby, Ed., 2000, Billings, MT: Newport Press).

In Text Citation Example

(Anders, 2001/2014)

Book with One Author, Ebook or Electronic Version

Anders, J. R. (2014). *Writing with style*. Retrieved from http://www.apamadeasy.com/ebooks

Book with One Author, No Date, Ebook or Electronic Version

Anders, J. R. (n.d.). *Writing with style*. Retrieved from http://www.apamadeasy.com/ebooks

Book with One Author, Ebook or Electronic Version, with DOI

Anders, J. R. (2014). *Writing with style*. doi:10.1234567890

Book with One Author, Ebook or Electronic Version, Republished Date - Use the latest date listed

Anders, J. R. (2014). *Writing with style*. Retrieved from http://www.apamadeasy.com/ebooks

Book with One Author, Ebook or Electronic Version, with DOI - Republished Date - Use the latest date listed

Anders, J. R. (2014). *Writing with style*. doi:10.1234567890

Book with One Author, Ebook or Electronic Version, Edition Other Than First

Anders, J. (2012). *APA made easy* (4th ed.). Retrieved from http://www.apamadeasy.com/ebooks

Book with One Author, Ebook or Electronic Version, Revised Edition

Anders, J. (2012). *APA made easy* (Rev. ed.). Retrieved from http://www.apamadeasy.com/ebooks

Book with One Author, Ebook or Electronic Version, Title with Subtitle

Anders, J. (2012). *APA made easy: Writing with style.* Retrieved from http://www.apamadeasy.com/ebooks

Book with One Author, Ebook or Electronic Version, No Date, Title with Subtitle

Anders, J. (n.d.). *APA made easy: Writing with style.* Retrieved from http://www.apamadeasy.com/ebooks

Book with One Author, Ebook or Electronic Version, Title with Proper Noun

Anders, J. (2014). *The life and times of J. Edgar Hoover.* Retrieved from http://www.apamadeasy.com/ebooks

Book with One Author, Ebook or Electronic Version, Title with Subtitle, Edition Other than First

Anders, J. (2014). *APA made easy: Writing with style* (4th ed.). Retrieved from http://www.apamadeasy.com/ebooks

Book with One Author, Ebook or Electronic Version, No Date, Title with Subtitle, Edition Other than First

Anders, J. (n.d.). *APA made easy: Writing with style* (4th ed.). Retrieved from http://www.apamadeasy.com/ebooks

Book with One Author, Ebook or Electronic Version, Title with Series

Anders, J. (2012). *APA made easy: Vol. 4. Writing with style.* Retrieved from http://www.apamadeasy.com/ebooks

Book with One Author, Electronic Version of Print Version from E-Reader (Kindle, Nook, etc.) - Type of Electronic version goes in brackets

Anders, J. A. (2014). *APA made easy* [Kindle version]. Retrieved from http://www.youversustheworld.com/asp

Book with One Author, Electronic Version of Republished Print Book

Anders, J. C. (2014). Writing in style. In R. Miller (Ed.), *Problem solving while writing long books* (pp. 80-88). Retrieved from http://www.youversustheworld.com/urlexamples (Original work published 2001)

Book with One Author, Electronic Version of Republished Print Book, No Page Numbers Available

Anders, J. C. (2014). Writing in style. In R. Miller (Ed.), *Problem solving while writing long books.* Retrieved from http://www.youversustheworld.com/urlexamples

Chapter in Electronic Book/Ebook with One Author

Anders, J. A. (2014). Writing in style. In R. Miller (Ed.), *Writing Fundamentals* (pp. 93-103). Retrieved from http://www.youversustheworld.com/chapterreferences

Chapter in Electronic Book/Ebook with One Author, with DOI

Anders, J. A. (2014). Writing in style. In R. Miller (Ed.), *Writing Fundamentals* (pp. 93-103). doi:10.1234567890

Chapter in Electronic Book/Ebook with One Author, Republished Date - Use the latest date listed

Anders, J. (2012). Writing in style. In R. Miller (Ed.), *APA made easy.* Retrieved from http://www.youversustheworld.com/chapterreferences

Chapter in Electronic Book/Ebook with One Author, Title with Subtitle

Anders, J. (2012). Writing in style. In R. Miller (Ed.), *APA made easy: A new way of formatting.* Retrieved from http://www.youversustheworld.com/chapterreferences

Chapter in Electronic Book/Ebook with One Author, Title with Subtitle, Republished Date - Use the latest date listed

Anders, J. (2012). Writing in style. In R. Miller (Ed.), *APA made easy: Writing with style.* Retrieved from http://www.youversustheworld.com/chapterreferences

Chapter in Electronic Book/Ebook of Print Version from Republished Book with One Author, with Volume Number

Anders, J. (2014). Creating a new metaphor. In R. McClure (Ed.). *Writing with style* (Vol. 1, pp. 105-144). Retrieved from http://www.youversustheworld.com/chapterreference

Chapter in Electronic Book/Ebook, English Translation, One Author

Anders, J. R. (2014). Creating a new metaphor (R. Miller, Trans.). In B. Reynolds (Ed.), *Formatting for dummies* (pp. 3-56). Retrieved from http://www.youversustheworld.com/chapterreferences

Chapter in Electronic Book/Ebook with One Author, Title with Proper Noun

Anders, J. (2014). Writing in style. In R. Miller (Ed.), *The life and times of J. Edgar Hoover.* Retrieved from http://www.youversustheworld.com/chapterreferences

Chapter in Electronic Book/Ebook with One Author, Limited Circulation, From Database - Include URL of database where chapter can be found

Anders, J. A. (2014). Writing in style. In R. Miller (Ed.), *Creating a new metaphor.* Retrieved from http://www.nameofonlinedatabaseurl.edu/onlinelimitedcirculation

Chapter in Electronic Book/Ebook, English Translation, One Author

Anders, J. R. (2014). Creating a new metaphor (R. Miller, Trans.). In B. Reynolds (Ed.), *Formatting for dummies* (pp. 3-56). Retrieved from http://www.youversustheworld.com/chapterreferences

Chapter in Electronic Book/Ebook, English Translation, One Author, Reprinted from Another Source

Anders, J. R. (2014). Creating a new metaphor (R. Miller, Trans.). In B. Reynolds (Ed.), *Formatting for dummies* (pp. 3-56). Retrieved from http://www.youversustheworld.com/chapterreferences (Reprinted from *Formatting for fun*, pp. 78-121, by B. B. Newby, Ed., 2000, Billings, MT: Newport Press).

Chapter in Electronic Book/Ebook of Print Version with One Author (Kindle, Nook, etc.)

Anders, J. (2014). Creating a new metaphor. In R. McClure (Ed.). *Writing with style* [iBooks version]. Retrieved from http://www.ibooks.com/chapterreferences

Chapter in Electronic Book/Ebook of Print Version with One Author, with DOI

Anders, J. (2014). Creating a new metaphor. In R. McClure (Ed.). *Writing with style* [iBooks version]. doi:10.1234567890

Reference Book with One Author - Only list Editor's Name

Anders, J. (Ed.). (2014). *References in obscurity.* Wauconda, IL: Anchor Press.

Entry in Reference Book with One Author

Anders, J. (2014). References in obscurity. In R. Miller (Ed.), *Getting references right* (3rd ed., Vol. 8). Wauconda, IL: Anchor Press.

Entry in Online Reference Book with One Author

Anders, J. (2014). References in obscurity. In R. Miller (Ed.), *Getting references right* (3rd ed., Vol. 8). Retrieved from http://www.youversustheworld.com/referencesbooks

Entry in Online Reference Book with One Author, with DOI

Anders, J. (2014). References in obscurity. In R. Miller (Ed.), *Getting references right* (3rd ed., Vol. 8). doi:10.1234567890

Entry in Online Reference Book with One Author, with Page Numbers, with DOI

Anders, J. (2014). References in obscurity. In R. Miller (Ed.), *Getting references right* (pp. 251-298). doi:10.1234567890

Entry in Online Reference Book with One Author, Alternative Edition Example

Anders, J. (2014). References in obscurity. In R. Miller (Ed.), *Getting references right* (Spring 2008 ed.). Retrieved from http://www.youversustheworld.com/referencesbooks

Books with Two Authors

A Quick Overview : **Books with Two Authors**

Sample Reference Structure:

First Author Last Name, First Author Initials., & Second Author Last Name, Second Author Initials. (Year of Publication). *Title of Publication.* City, State Initials: Publisher.

Example:

Anders, J., & Beiler, R. (2012). *APA made easy.* New York, NY: Anchor Press.

Electronic Sample

First Author Last Name, First Author Initials., & Second Author Last Name, Second Author Initials. (Year of Publication). *Title of Publication.* Retrieved from http://nameofurl.com

Electronic Example

Anders, J. T., & Beiler, R. M. (2014). *Writing with style.* Retrieved from http://www.apamadeasy.com/ebooks

Sample In-Text Citations

Example #1: Paraphrase

There have been cases where people have compared Anders and Bieler's book (2012) to *APA Made Easy* because of the similarities in writing style.

Example #2: Paraphrase

Easy APA Formatting (Anders & Bieler, 2012) has been compared to APA Made Easy.

Example #3: Direct Quote

The book on Fairy Tales was described as "a wonderful tale of hope and dreams" (Anders & Bieler, 2012, p.19).

Books with Two Authors

Book with Two Authors, Standard Date of Publication

Anders, J., & Beiler, R. (2012). *APA made easy*. New York, NY: Anchor Press.

Book with Two Authors, No Date

Anders, J., & Beiler, R. (n.d.). *APA made easy.* New York, NY: Anchor Press.

Book with Two Authors, Republished Date - Use the latest date listed

Anders, J., & Beiler, R. (2012). *APA made easy*. New York, NY: Anchor Press.

In Text Citation Example - Cite both the original published date and the date of the republished version:
(Anders & Beiler, 2000/2014).

Book with Two Authors, Edition Other Than First

Anders, J., & Beiler, R. (2012). *APA made easy* (4th ed.). New York, NY: Anchor Press.

Book with Two Authors, Revised Edition

Anders, J., & Beiler, R. (2012). *APA made easy* (Rev. ed.). New York, NY: Anchor Press.

Book with Two Authors, Title with Subtitle

Anders, J., & Beiler, R. (2012). *APA made easy: Writing with style.* New York, NY: Anchor Press.

Book with Two Authors, No Date, Title with Subtitle

Anders, J., & Beiler, R. (n.d.). *APA made easy: Writing with style.* New York, NY: Anchor Press.

Book with Two Authors, Title with Proper Noun

Anders, J., & Beiler, R. (2014). *The life and times of J. Edgar Hoover.* New York, NY: Anchor Press.

Book with Two Authors with Hyphenated Name

Anders, J.-R., & Beiler, R. (2014). *The life and times of J. Edgar Hoover.* New York, NY: Anchor Press.

Book with Two Authors, Title with Subtitle, Edition Other than First

Anders, J., & Beiler, R. (2014). *APA made easy: Writing with style* (4th ed.). New York, NY: Anchor Press.

Book with Two Authors, No Date, Title with Subtitle, Edition Other than First

Anders, J., & Beiler, R. (n.d.). *APA made easy: Writing with style* (4th ed.). New York, NY: Anchor Press.

Book with Two Authors, Title with Series

Anders, J., & Beiler, R. (2012). *APA made easy: Vol. 4. Writing with style.* New York, NY: Anchor Press.

Book with Two Authors, Limited Circulation, Not Online

Anders, J. A., & Beiler, R. M. (2014). *Creating a new metaphor.* (Available from Baker, 122 South Salem Street, Billings, MT. 59101)

Book with Two Authors, Limited Circulation, From Database

Anders, J. A., & Beiler, R. M. (2014). *Creating a new metaphor.* Retrieved from http://www.nameofonlinedatabaseurl.edu/onlinelimitedcirculation

Book with Two Authors, Monograph

Anders, J. A., & Beiler, R. M. (2014). *Creating a new metaphor* [Monograph]. Retrieved from http://www.nameofonlinedatabaseurl.edu/onlinelimitedcirculation

Book with Two Authors, No Date, Monograph

Anders, J. A., & Beiler, R. M. (n.d.). *Creating a new metaphor* [Monograph]. Retrieved from http://www.nameofonlinedatabaseurl.edu/onlinelimitedcirculation

Chapter in Book with Two Authors

Anders, J. A., & Beiler, R. M. (2014). Writing in style. In R. Miller (Ed.), *Writing Fundamentals* (pp. 93-103). New York, NY: Anchor Press.

Chapter in Book with Two Authors, Republished Date - Use the latest date listed

Anders, J., & Beiler, R. (2012). Writing in style. In R. Miller (Ed.), *APA made easy*. New York, NY: Anchor Press.

Chapter in Book with Two Authors, Title with Subtitle

Anders, J., & Beiler, R. (2012). Writing in style. In R. Miller (Ed.), *APA made easy: A new way of formatting*. New York, NY: Anchor Press.

Chapter in Book, English Translation, Two Authors

Anders, J. T., & Beiler, R. M. (2014). Creating a new metaphor (R. Miller, Trans.). In B. Reynolds (Ed.), *Formatting for dummies* (pp. 3-56). Dallas, TX: Anchor Press.

Chapter in Book with Two Authors, Title with Proper Noun

Anders, J., & Beiler, R. (2014). Writing in style. In R. Miller (Ed.), *The life and times of J. Edgar Hoover*. New York, NY: Anchor Press.

Chapter in Book with Two Authors, Limited Circulation, Not Online

Anders, J. A., & Beiler, R. M. (2014). Writing in style. In R. Miller (Ed.), *Creating a new metaphor*. (Available from Baker, 122 South Salem Street, Billings, MT. 59101)

Chapter in Book with Two Authors, Limited Circulation, From Database - include URL of database where chapter can be found

Anders, J. A., & Beiler, R. M. (2014). Writing in style. In R. Miller (Ed.), *Creating a new metaphor*. Retrieved from http://www.nameofonlinedatabaseurl.edu/onlinelimitedcirculation

Chapter in Book, English Translation, Two Authors

Anders, J. T., & Beiler, R. M. (2014). Creating a new metaphor (R. Miller, Trans.). In B. Reynolds (Ed.), *Formatting for dummies* (pp. 3-56). Dallas, TX: Anchor Press.

Chapter in Book, English Translation, Two Authors, Reprinted from Another Source

Anders, J. T., & Beiler, R. M. (2014). Creating a new metaphor (R. Miller, Trans.). In B. Reynolds (Ed.), *Formatting for dummies* (pp. 3-56). Dallas, TX: Anchor Press. (Reprinted from *Formatting for fun*, pp. 78-121, by B. B. Newby, Ed., 2000, Billings, MT: Newport Press).

Book with Two Authors, Ebook or Electronic Version

Anders, J. T., & Beiler, R. M. (2014). *Writing with style.* Retrieved from http://www.apamadeasy.com/ebooks

Book with Two Authors, No Date, Ebook or Electronic Version

Anders, J. T., & Beiler, R. M. (n.d.). *Writing with style.* Retrieved from http://www.apamadeasy.com/ebooks

Book with Two Authors, Ebook or Electronic Version, with DOI

Anders, J. T., & Beiler, R. M. (2014). *Writing with style.* doi:10.1234567890

Book with Two Authors, Ebook or Electronic Version, Republished Date - Use the latest date listed

Anders, J. T., & Beiler, R. M. (2014). *Writing with style.* Retrieved from http://www.apamadeasy.com/ebooks

Book with Two Authors, Ebook or Electronic Version, with DOI - Republished Date - Use the latest date listed

Anders, J. T., & Beiler, R. M. (2014). *Writing with style.* doi:10.1234567890

Book with Two Authors, Ebook or Electronic Version, Edition Other Than First

Anders, J., & Beiler, R. (2012). *APA made easy* (4th ed.). Retrieved from http://www.apamadeasy.com/ebooks

Book with Two Authors, Ebook or Electronic Version, Revised Edition

Anders, J., & Beiler, R. (2012). *APA made easy* (Rev. ed.). Retrieved from http://www.apamadeasy.com/ebooks

Book with Two Authors, Ebook or Electronic Version, Title with Subtitle

Anders, J., & Beiler, R. (2012). *APA made easy: Writing with style.* Retrieved from http://www.apamadeasy.com/ebooks

Book with Two Authors, Ebook or Electronic Version, No Date, Title with Subtitle

Anders, J., & Beiler, R. (n.d.). *APA made easy: Writing with style.* Retrieved from http://www.apamadeasy.com/ebooks

Book with Two Authors, Ebook or Electronic Version, Title with Proper Noun

Anders, J., & Beiler, R. (2014). *The life and times of J. Edgar Hoover.* Retrieved from http://www.apamadeasy.com/ebooks

Book with Two Authors, Ebook or Electronic Version, Title with Subtitle, Edition Other than First

Anders, J., & Beiler, R. (2014). *APA made easy: Writing with style* (4th ed.). Retrieved from http://www.apamadeasy.com/ebooks

Book with Two Authors, Ebook or Electronic Version, No Date, Title with Subtitle, Edition Other than First

Anders, J., & Beiler, R. (n.d.). *APA made easy: Writing with style* (4th ed.). Retrieved from http://www.apamadeasy.com/ebooks

Book with Two Authors, Ebook or Electronic Version, Title with Series

Anders, J., & Beiler, R. (2012). *APA made easy: Vol. 4. Writing with style.* Retrieved from http://www.apamadeasy.com/ebooks

Book with Two Authors, Electronic Version of Print Version from E-Reader (Kindle, Nook, etc.) - Type of Electronic version goes in brackets

Anders, J. A., & Beiler, R. M. (2014). *APA made easy* [Kindle version]. Retrieved from http://www.youversustheworld.com/asp

Book with Two Authors, Electronic Version of Republished Print Book

Anders, J., & Beiler, R. (2014). Writing in style. In R. Miller (Ed.), *Problem solving while writing long books* (pp. 80-88). Retrieved from http://www.youversustheworld.com/urlexamples (Original work published 2001)

Book with Two Authors, Electronic Version of Republished Print Book, No Page Numbers Available

Anders, J., & Beiler, R. (2014). Writing in style. In R. Miller (Ed.), *Problem solving while writing long books*. Retrieved from http://www.youversustheworld.com/urlexamples

Chapter in Electronic Book/Ebook with Two Authors

Anders, J. A., & Beiler, R. M. (2014). Writing in style. In R. Miller (Ed.), *Writing Fundamentals* (pp. 93-103). Retrieved from http://www.youversustheworld.com/chapterreferences

Chapter in Electronic Book/Ebook with Two Authors, with DOI

Anders, J. A., & Beiler, R. M. (2014). Writing in style. In R. Miller (Ed.), *Writing Fundamentals* (pp. 93-103). doi:10.1234567890

Chapter in Electronic Book/Ebook with Two Authors, Republished Date - Use the latest date listed

Anders, J., & Beiler, R. (2012). Writing in style. In R. Miller (Ed.), *APA made easy*. Retrieved from http://www.youversustheworld.com/chapterreferences

Chapter in Electronic Book/Ebook with Two Authors, Title with Subtitle

Anders, J., & Beiler, R. (2012). Writing in style. In R. Miller (Ed.), *APA made easy: A new way of formatting*. Retrieved from http://www.youversustheworld.com/chapterreferences

Chapter in Electronic Book/Ebook with Two Authors, Title with Subtitle, Republished Date - Use the latest date listed

Anders, J., & Beiler, R. (2012). Writing in style. In R. Miller (Ed.), *APA made easy: Writing with style*. Retrieved from http://www.youversustheworld.com/chapterreferences

Chapter in Electronic Book/Ebook of Print Version from Republished Book with Two Authors, with Volume Number

Anders, J., & Beiler, R. (2014). Creating a new metaphor. In R. McClure (Ed.). *Writing with style* (Vol. 1, pp. 105-144). Retrieved from http://www.youversustheworld.com/chapterreference

Chapter in Electronic Book/Ebook, English Translation, Two Authors

Anders, J. T., & Beiler, R. M. (2014). Creating a new metaphor (R. Miller, Trans.). In B. Reynolds (Ed.), *Formatting for dummies* (pp. 3-56). Retrieved from http://www.youversustheworld.com/chapterreferences

Chapter in Electronic Book/Ebook with Two Authors, Title with Proper Noun

Anders, J., & Beiler, R. (2014). Writing in style. In R. Miller (Ed.), *The life and times of J. Edgar Hoover.* Retrieved from http://www.youversustheworld.com/chapterreferences

Chapter in Electronic Book/Ebook with Two Authors, Limited Circulation, From Database - Include URL of database where chapter can be found

Anders, J. A., & Beiler, R. M. (2014). Writing in style. In R. Miller (Ed.), *Creating a new metaphor.* Retrieved from http://www.nameofonlinedatabaseurl.edu/onlinelimitedcirculation

Chapter in Electronic Book/Ebook, English Translation, Two Authors

Anders, J. T., & Beiler, R. M. (2014). Creating a new metaphor (R. Miller, Trans.). In B. Reynolds (Ed.), *Formatting for dummies* (pp. 3-56). Retrieved from http://www.youversustheworld.com/chapterreferences

Chapter in Electronic Book/Ebook, English Translation, Two Authors, Reprinted from Another Source

Anders, J. T., & Beiler, R. M. (2014). Creating a new metaphor (R. Miller, Trans.). In B. Reynolds (Ed.), *Formatting for dummies* (pp. 3-56). Retrieved from http://www.youversustheworld.com/chapterreferences (Reprinted from *Formatting for fun*, pp. 78-121, by B. B. Newby, Ed., 2000, Billings, MT: Newport Press).

Chapter in Electronic Book/Ebook of Print Version with Two Authors (Kindle, Nook, etc.)

Anders, J., & Beiler, R. (2014). Creating a new metaphor. In R. McClure (Ed.). *Writing with style* [iBooks version]. Retrieved from http://www.ibooks.com/chapterreferences

Chapter in Electronic Book/Ebook of Print Version with Two Authors, with DOI

Anders, J., & Beiler, R. (2014). Creating a new metaphor. In R. McClure (Ed.). *Writing with style* [iBooks version]. doi:10.1234567890

Reference Book with Two Authors - Only list Editor's Name

Anders, J., & Beiler, R. (Ed.). (2014). *References in obscurity.* Wauconda, IL: Anchor Press.

Entry in Reference Book with Two Authors

Anders, J., & Beiler, R. (2014). References in obscurity. In R. Miller (Ed.), *Getting references right* (3rd ed., Vol. 8). Wauconda, IL: Anchor Press.

Entry in Online Reference Book with Two Authors

Anders, J., & Beiler, R. (2014). References in obscurity. In R. Miller (Ed.), *Getting references right* (3rd ed., Vol. 8). Retrieved from http://www.youversustheworld.com/referencesbooks

Entry in Online Reference Book with Two Authors, with DOI

Anders, J., & Beiler, R. (2014). References in obscurity. In R. Miller (Ed.), *Getting references right* (3rd ed., Vol. 8). doi:10.1234567890

Entry in Online Reference Book with Two Authors, with Page Numbers, with DOI

Anders, J., & Beiler, R. (2014). References in obscurity. In R. Miller (Ed.), *Getting references right* (pp. 251-298). doi:10.1234567890

Entry in Online Reference Book with Two Authors, Alternative Edition

Example

Anders, J., & Beiler, R. (2014). References in obscurity. In R. Miller (Ed.), *Getting references right* (Spring 2008 ed.). Retrieved from http://www.youversustheworld.com/referencesbooks

Books with Three Authors

A Quick Overview : **Books with Three Authors**

Sample Reference Structure:

Last Name, First Initial., Second Last Name, First Initial., & Third Last Name, Third First Initial. (Date of Publication). *Title of work.* Location City, State Initial: Publisher.

Example:

Anders, J., Smith, D. R., & Rohn, R. (2012). *APA made easy*. New York, NY: Anchor Press.

Electronic Sample

Last Name, First Initial., Second Last Name, Second First Initial., & Third Last Name, Third First Initial. (Date of Publication). *Title of work.* Retrieved from http://nameofurl.com

Electronic Example

Anders, J., Smith, P., & Rohn, R. (2014). *Writing with style*. Retrieved from http://www.apamadeasy.com/ebooks

Sample In-Text Citations

For your first time citing a book with three authors, your in text citation should appear like this:
(Smith, Johnson, & Zeigler, 2013)

For subsequent paragraph citation after the first
(Smith et al., 2013)

Every subsequent citation omits the year:
(Smith et al.)

Example #1: Paraphrase
There have been cases where people have compared Smith, Johnson, and Zeigler (2012) to *APA Made Easy* because of the similarities in writing style.

Example #2: Paraphrase
Smith et al. (2012) have compared to APA formatting to MLA formatting.

Example #3: Second Instance of Paraphrase

Smith et al. have compared to APA formatting to MLA formatting.

Example #4: Direct Quote

The book on Fairy Tales was described as "a wonderful tale of hope and dreams" (Smith, Johnson, & Zeigler, 2012, p. 9).

Example #5: Direct Quote, Second Instance

The book on Fairy Tales was described as "a wonderful tale of hope and dreams" (Smith et al., 2012, p. 9).

Books with Three Authors

Book with Three Authors, Standard Date of Publication

Anders, J., Smith, D. R., & Rohn, R. (2012). *APA made easy.* New York, NY: Anchor Press.

Book with Three Authors, No Date

Anders, J., Smith, D. R., & Rohn, R. (n.d.). *APA made easy.* New York, NY: Anchor Press.

Book with Three Authors, Republished Date - Use the latest date listed

Anders, J., Smith, D. R., & Rohn, R. (2012). *APA made easy.* New York, NY: Anchor Press.

In Text Citation Example - Cite both the original published date and the date of the republished version:

(Anders, Smith, & Robin, 2000/2012).

Book with Three Authors, Edition Other Than First

Anders, J., Smith, D. R., & Rohn, R. (2012). *APA made easy* (4th ed.). New York, NY: Anchor Press.

Book with Three Authors, Revised Edition

Anders, J., Smith, D. R., & Rohn, R. (2012). *APA made easy* (Rev. ed.). New York, NY: Anchor Press.

Book with Three Authors, Title with Subtitle

Anders, J., Smith, D. R., & Rohn, R. (2012). *APA made easy: Writing with style.* New York, NY: Anchor Press.

Book with Three Authors, No Date, Title with Subtitle

Anders, J., Smith, D. R., & Rohn, R. (n.d.). *APA made easy: Writing with style.* New York, NY: Anchor Press.

Book with Three Authors, Title with Proper Noun

Anders, J., Smith, D. R., & Rohn, R. (2014). *The life and times of J. Edgar Hoover.* New York, NY: Anchor Press.

Book with Three Authors, Title with Subtitle, Edition Other than First

Anders, J., Smith, D. R., & Rohn, R. (2014). *APA made easy: Writing with style* (4th ed.). New York, NY: Anchor Press.

Book with Three Authors, No Date, Title with Subtitle, Edition Other than First

Anders, J., Smith, D. R., & Rohn, R. (n.d.). *APA made easy: Writing with style* (4th ed.). New York, NY: Anchor Press.

Book with Three Authors, Title with Series

Anders, J., Smith, D. R., & Rohn, R. (2012). *APA made easy: Vol. 4. Writing with style.* New York, NY: Anchor Press.

Book with Three Authors, Limited Circulation, Not Online

Anders, J., Smith, P., & Rogers, R. (2014). *Creating a new metaphor.* (Available from Baker, 122 South Salem Street, Billings, MT. 59101)

Book with Three Authors, Limited Circulation, From Database

Anders, J., Smith, P., & Rogers, R. (2014). *Creating a new metaphor.* Retrieved from http://www.nameofonlinedatabaseurl.edu/onlinelimitedcirculation

Book with Three Authors, Monograph

Anders, J., Smith, P., & Rogers, R. (2014). *Creating a new metaphor* [Monograph]. Retrieved from http://www.nameofonlinedatabaseurl.edu/onlinelimitedcirculation

Book with Three Authors, No Date, Monograph

Anders, J., Smith, P., & Rogers, R. (n.d.). *Creating a new metaphor* [Monograph]. Retrieved from http://www.nameofonlinedatabaseurl.edu/onlinelimitedcirculation

Chapter in Book with Three Authors

Anders, J., Smith, P., & Rogers, R. (2014). Writing in style. In R. Miller (Ed.), *Writing Fundamentals* (pp. 93-103). New York, NY: Anchor Press.

Chapter in Book with Three Authors, Republished Date - Use the latest date listed

Anders, J., Smith, D. R., & Rohn, R. (2012). Writing in style. In R. Miller (Ed.), *APA made easy*. New York, NY: Anchor Press.

Chapter in Book with Three Authors, Title with Subtitle

Anders, J., Smith, D. R., & Rohn, R. (2012). Writing in style. In R. Miller (Ed.), *APA made easy: A new way of formatting*. New York, NY: Anchor Press.

Chapter in Book, English Translation, Three Authors

Anders, J., Smith, P., & Rohn, R. (2014). Creating a new metaphor (R. Miller, Trans.). In B. Reynolds (Ed.), *Formatting for dummies* (pp. 3-56). Dallas, TX: Anchor Press.

Chapter in Book with Three Authors, Title with Proper Noun

Anders, J., Smith, D. R., & Rohn, R. (2014). Writing in style. In R. Miller (Ed.), *The life and times of J. Edgar Hoover*. New York, NY: Anchor Press.

Book with Three Authors with Hyphenated Name

Anders, J.-R., Smith, D. R., & Rohn, R. (2014). *The life and times of J. Edgar Hoover*. New York, NY: Anchor Press.

Chapter in Book with Three Authors, Limited Circulation, Not Online

Anders, J., Smith, P., & Rogers, R. (2014). Writing in style. In R. Miller (Ed.), *Creating a new metaphor*. (Available from Baker, 122 South Salem Street, Billings, MT. 59101)

Chapter in Book with Three Authors, Limited Circulation, From Database - include URL of database where chapter can be found

Anders, J., Smith, P., & Rogers, R. (2014). Writing in style. In R. Miller (Ed.), *Creating a new metaphor*. Retrieved from http://www.nameofonlinedatabaseurl.edu/onlinelimitedcirculation

Chapter in Book, English Translation, Three Authors

Anders, J., Smith, P., & Rohn, R. (2014). Creating a new metaphor (R. Miller, Trans.). In B. Reynolds (Ed.), *Formatting for dummies* (pp. 3-56). Dallas, TX: Anchor Press.

Chapter in Book, English Translation, Three Authors, Reprinted from Another Source

Anders, J., Smith, P., & Rohn, R. (2014). Creating a new metaphor (R. Miller, Trans.). In B. Reynolds (Ed.), *Formatting for dummies* (pp. 3-56). Dallas, TX: Anchor Press. (Reprinted from *Formatting for fun*, pp. 78-121, by B. B. Newby, Ed., 2000, Billings, MT: Newport Press).

Book with Three Authors, Ebook or Electronic Version

Anders, J., Smith, P., & Rohn, R. (2014). *Writing with style*. Retrieved from http://www.apamadeasy.com/ebooks

Book with Three Authors, No Date, Ebook or Electronic Version

Anders, J., Smith, P., & Rohn, R. (n.d.). *Writing with style*. Retrieved from http://www.apamadeasy.com/ebooks

Book with Three Authors, Ebook or Electronic Version, with DOI

Anders, J., Smith, P., & Rohn, R. (2014). *Writing with style*. doi:10.1234567890

Book with Three Authors, Ebook or Electronic Version, with DOI - Republished Date - Use the latest date listed

Anders, J., Smith, P., & Rohn, R. (2014). *Writing with style*. doi:10.1234567890

Book with Three Authors, Ebook or Electronic Version, Republished Date - Use the latest date listed

Anders, J., Smith, P., & Rohn, R. (2014). *Writing with style.* Retrieved from http://www.apamadeasy.com/ebooks

Book with Three Authors, Ebook or Electronic Version, Edition Other Than First

Anders, J., Smith, D. R., & Rohn, R. (2012). *APA made easy* (4th ed.). Retrieved from http://www.apamadeasy.com/ebooks

Book with Three Authors, Ebook or Electronic Version, Revised Edition

Anders, J., Smith, D. R., & Rohn, R. (2012). *APA made easy* (Rev. ed.). Retrieved from http://www.apamadeasy.com/ebooks

Book with Three Authors, Ebook or Electronic Version, Title with Subtitle

Anders, J., Smith, D. R., & Rohn, R. (2012). *APA made easy: Writing with style.* Retrieved from http://www.apamadeasy.com/ebooks

Book with Three Authors, Ebook or Electronic Version, No Date, Title with Subtitle

Anders, J., Smith, D. R., & Rohn, R. (n.d.). *APA made easy: Writing with style.* Retrieved from http://www.apamadeasy.com/ebooks

Book with Three Authors, Ebook or Electronic Version, Title with Proper Noun

Anders, J., Smith, D. R., & Rohn, R. (2014). *The life and times of J. Edgar Hoover.* Retrieved from http://www.apamadeasy.com/ebooks

Book with Three Authors, Ebook or Electronic Version, Title with Subtitle, Edition Other than First

Anders, J., Smith, D. R., & Rohn, R. (2014). *APA made easy: Writing with style* (4th ed.). Retrieved from http://www.apamadeasy.com/ebooks

Book with Three Authors, Ebook or Electronic Version, No Date, Title with Subtitle, Edition Other than First

Anders, J., Smith, D. R., & Rohn, R. (n.d.). *APA made easy: Writing with style* (4th ed.). Retrieved from http://www.apamadeasy.com/ebooks

Book with Three Authors, Ebook or Electronic Version, Title with Series

Anders, J., Smith, D. R., & Rohn, R. (2012). *APA made easy: Vol. 4. Writing with style.* Retrieved from http://www.apamadeasy.com/ebooks

Book with Three Authors, Electronic Version of Print Version from E-Reader (Kindle, Nook, etc.) - Type of Electronic version goes in brackets

Anders, J., Smith, P., & Rogers, R. (2014). *APA made easy* [Kindle version]. Retrieved from http://www.youversustheworld.com/asp

Book with Three Authors, Electronic Version of Republished Print Book

Anders, J., Smith, D. R., & Rohn, R. (2014). Writing in style. In R. Miller (Ed.), *Problem solving while writing long books* (pp. 80-88). Retrieved from http://www.youversustheworld.com/urlexamples (Original work published 2001)

Book with Three Authors, Electronic Version of Republished Print Book, No Page Numbers Available

Anders, J., Smith, D. R., & Rohn, R. (2014). Writing in style. In R. Miller (Ed.), *Problem solving while writing long books*. Retrieved from http://www.youversustheworld.com/urlexamples

Chapter in Electronic Book/Ebook with Three Authors

Anders, J., Smith, P., & Rogers, R. (2014). Writing in style. In R. Miller (Ed.), *Writing Fundamentals* (pp. 93-103). Retrieved from http://www.youversustheworld.com/chapterreferences

Chapter in Electronic Book/Ebook with Three Authors, with DOI

Anders, J., Smith, P., & Rogers, R. (2014). Writing in style. In R. Miller (Ed.), *Writing Fundamentals* (pp. 93-103). doi:10.1234567890

Chapter in Electronic Book/Ebook with Three Authors, Republished Date - Use the latest date listed

Anders, J., Smith, D. R., & Rohn, R. (2012). Writing in style. In R. Miller (Ed.), *APA made easy*. Retrieved from http://www.youversustheworld.com/chapterreferences

Chapter in Electronic Book/Ebook with Three Authors, Title with Subtitle

Anders, J., Smith, D. R., & Rohn, R. (2012). Writing in style. In R. Miller (Ed.), *APA made easy: A new way of formatting*. Retrieved from http://www.youversustheworld.com/chapterreferences

Chapter in Electronic Book/Ebook with Three Authors, Title with Subtitle, Republished Date - Use the latest date listed

Anders, J., Smith, D. R., & Rohn, R. (2012). Writing in style. In R. Miller (Ed.), *APA made easy: Writing with style*. Retrieved from http://www.youversustheworld.com/chapterreferences

Chapter in Electronic Book/Ebook of Print Version from Republished Book with Three Authors, with Volume Number

Anders, J., Smith, D. R., & Rohn, R. (2014). Creating a new metaphor. In R. McClure (Ed.). *Writing with style* (Vol. 1, pp. 105-144). Retrieved from http://www.youversustheworld.com/chapterreference

Chapter in Electronic Book/Ebook, English Translation, Three Authors

Anders, J., Smith, P., & Rohn, R. (2014). Creating a new metaphor (R. Miller, Trans.). In B. Reynolds (Ed.), *Formatting for dummies* (pp. 3-56). Retrieved from http://www.youversustheworld.com/chapterreferences

Chapter in Electronic Book/Ebook with Three Authors, Title with Proper Noun

Anders, J., Smith, D. R., & Rohn, R. (2014). Writing in style. In R. Miller (Ed.), *The life and times of J. Edgar Hoover*. Retrieved from http://www.youversustheworld.com/chapterreferences

Chapter in Electronic Book/Ebook with Three Authors, Limited Circulation, From Database - Include URL of database where chapter can be found

Anders, J., Smith, P., & Rogers, R. (2014). Writing in style. In R. Miller (Ed.), *Creating a new metaphor*. Retrieved from http://www.nameofonlinedatabaseurl.edu/onlinelimitedcirculation

Chapter in Electronic Book/Ebook, English Translation, Three Authors

Anders, J., Smith, P., & Rohn, R. (2014). Creating a new metaphor (R. Miller, Trans.). In B. Reynolds (Ed.), *Formatting for dummies* (pp. 3-56). Retrieved from http://www.youversustheworld.com/chapterreferences

Chapter in Electronic Book/Ebook, English Translation, Three Authors, Reprinted from Another Source

Anders, J., Smith, P., & Rohn, R. (2014). Creating a new metaphor (R. Miller, Trans.). In B. Reynolds (Ed.), *Formatting for dummies* (pp. 3-56). Retrieved from http://www.youversustheworld.com/chapterreferences (Reprinted from *Formatting for fun*, pp. 78-121, by B. B. Newby, Ed., 2000, Billings, MT: Newport Press).

Chapter in Electronic Book/Ebook of Print Version with Three Authors (Kindle, Nook, etc.)

Anders, J., Smith, D. R., & Rohn, R. (2014). Creating a new metaphor. In R. McClure (Ed.). *Writing with style* [iBooks version]. Retrieved from http://www.ibooks.com/chapterreferences

Chapter in Electronic Book/Ebook of Print Version with Three Authors, with DOI

Anders, J., Smith, D. R., & Rohn, R. (2014). Creating a new metaphor. In R. McClure (Ed.). *Writing with style* [iBooks version]. doi:10.1234567890

Reference Book with Three Authors - Only list Editor's Name

Anders, J., Smith, D. R., & Rohn, R. (Ed.). (2014). *References in obscurity*. Wauconda, IL: Anchor Press.

Entry in Reference Book with Three Authors

Anders, J., Smith, D. R., & Rohn, R. (2014). References in obscurity. In R. Miller (Ed.), *Getting references right* (3rd ed., Vol. 8). Wauconda, IL: Anchor Press.

Entry in Online Reference Book with Three Authors

Anders, J., Smith, D. R., & Rohn, R. (2014). References in obscurity. In R. Miller (Ed.), *Getting references right* (3rd ed., Vol. 8). Retrieved from http://www.youversustheworld.com/referencesbooks

Entry in Online Reference Book with Three Authors, with DOI

Anders, J., Smith, D. R., & Rohn, R. (2014). References in obscurity. In R. Miller (Ed.), *Getting references right* (3rd ed., Vol. 8). doi:10.1234567890

Entry in Online Reference Book with Three Authors, with Page Numbers, with DOI

Anders, J., Smith, D. R., & Rohn, R. (2014). References in obscurity. In R. Miller (Ed.), *Getting references right* (pp. 251-298). doi:10.1234567890

Entry in Online Reference Book with Three Authors, Alternative Edition Example

Anders, J., Smith, D. R., & Rohn, R. (2014). References in obscurity. In R. Miller (Ed.), *Getting references right* (Spring 2008 ed.). Retrieved from http://www.youversustheworld.com/referencesbooks

Books with Four Authors

A Quick Overview : **Books with Four Authors**

Sample Reference Structure:

Last Name, First Initial., Second Last Name, First Initial., Third Last Name, Third First Initial., & Fourth Last Name, Fourth First Initial. (Date of Publication). *Title of publication.* City, State Initials of Publication: Publisher.

Example:

Anders, J., Rossier, R. A., Swarinski, H., & Peters, B. (2012). *APA made easy*. New York, NY: Anchor Press.

Electronic Sample

Last Name, First Initial., Second Last Name, First Initial., Third Last Name, Third First Initial., & Fourth Last Name, Fourth First Initial. (Date of Publication). *Title of publication.* Retrieved from http://nameofurl.com

Electronic Example

Anders, J., Matkovich, R. A., Swarinski, H., & Peters, B. (2014). *Writing with style*. Retrieved from http://www.apamadeasy.com/ebooks

Sample In-Text Citations

For your first time citing a book with four authors, your in text citation should appear like this:
(Smith, Johnson, Hadden, & Zeigler, 2013)

For subsequent paragraph citation after the first
(Smith et al., 2013)

Every subsequent citation omits the year:
(Smith et al.)

Example #1: Paraphrase
There have been cases where people have compared Smith, Johnson, Hadden, and Zeigler (2012) to *APA Made Easy* because of the similarities in writing style.

Example #2: Paraphrase
Smith et al. (2012) have compared to APA formatting to MLA formatting.

Example #3: Second Instance of Paraphrase
Smith et al. have compared to APA formatting to MLA formatting.

Example #4: Direct Quote
The book on Fairy Tales was described as "a wonderful tale of hope and dreams" (Smith, Johnson, Haden & Zeigler, 2012, p. 29).

Example #5: Direct Quote, Second Instance
The book on Fairy Tales was described as "a wonderful tale of hope and dreams" (Smith et al., 2012, p. 29).

Books with Four Authors

Book with Four Authors, Standard Date of Publication

Anders, J., Rossier, R. A., Swarinski, H., & Peters, B. (2012). *APA made easy.* New York, NY: Anchor Press.

Book with Four Authors, No Date

Anders, J., Rossier, R. A., Swarinski, H., & Peters, B. (n.d.). *APA made easy.* New York, NY: Anchor Press.

Book with Four Authors, Republished Date - Use the latest date listed

Anders, J., Rossier, R. A., Swarinski, H., & Peters, B. (2012). *APA made easy.* New York, NY: Anchor Press.

In Text Citation Example - Cite both the original published date and the date of the republished version:
(Anders, Rossier, Swarinski, & Peters, 2000/2012).

Book with Four Authors, Edition Other Than First

Anders, J., Rossier, R. A., Swarinski, H., & Peters, B. (2012). *APA made easy* (4th ed.). New York, NY: Anchor Press.

Book with Four Authors, Revised Edition

Anders, J., Rossier, R. A., Swarinski, H., & Peters, B. (2012). *APA made easy* (Rev. ed.). New York, NY: Anchor Press.

Book with Four Authors, Title with Subtitle

Anders, J., Rossier, R. A., Swarinski, H., & Peters, B. (2012). *APA made easy: Writing with style.* New York, NY: Anchor Press.

Book with Four Authors, No Date, Title with Subtitle

Anders, J., Rossier, R. A., Swarinski, H., & Peters, B. (n.d.). *APA made easy: Writing with style.* New York, NY: Anchor Press.

Book with Four Authors, Title with Proper Noun

Anders, J., Rossier, R. A., Swarinski, H., & Peters, B. (2014). *The life and times of J. Edgar Hoover.* New York, NY: Anchor Press.

Book with Four Authors, Title with Subtitle, Edition Other than First

Anders, J., Rossier, R. A., Swarinski, H., & Peters, B. (2014). *APA made easy: Writing with style* (4th ed.). New York, NY: Anchor Press.

Book with Four Authors, No Date, Title with Subtitle, Edition Other than First

Anders, J., Rossier, R. A., Swarinski, H., & Peters, B. (n.d.). *APA made easy: Writing with style* (4th ed.). New York, NY: Anchor Press.

Book with Four Authors, Title with Series

Anders, J., Rossier, R. A., Swarinski, H., & Peters, B. (2012). *APA made easy: Vol. 4. Writing with style.* New York, NY: Anchor Press.

Book with Four Authors, Limited Circulation, Not Online

Anders, J., Matkovich, R. A., Swarinski, H., & Peters, B. (2014). *Creating a new metaphor.* (Available from Baker, 122 South Salem Street, Billings, MT. 59101)

Book with Four Authors, Limited Circulation, From Database

Anders, J., Matkovich, R. A., Swarinski, H., & Peters, B. (2014). *Creating a new metaphor.* Retrieved from http://www.nameofonlinedatabaseurl.edu/onlinelimitedcirculation

Book with Four Authors, Monograph

Anders, J., Matkovich, R. A., Swarinski, H., & Peters, B. (2014). *Creating a new metaphor* [Monograph]. Retrieved from http://www.nameofonlinedatabaseurl.edu/onlinelimitedcirculation

Book with Four Authors, No Date, Monograph

Anders, J., Matkovich, R. A., Swarinski, H., & Peters, B. (n.d.). *Creating a new metaphor* [Monograph]. Retrieved from http://www.nameofonlinedatabaseurl.edu/onlinelimitedcirculation

Chapter in Book with Four Authors

Anders, J., Matkovich, R. A., Swarinski, H., & Peters, B. (2014). Writing in style. In R. Miller (Ed.), *Writing Fundamentals* (pp. 93-103). New York, NY: Anchor Press.

Chapter in Book with Four Authors, Republished Date - Use the latest date listed

Anders, J., Rossier, R. A., Swarinski, H., & Peters, B. (2012). Writing in style. In R. Miller (Ed.), *APA made easy.* New York, NY: Anchor Press.

Chapter in Book with Four Authors, Title with Subtitle

Anders, J., Rossier, R. A., Swarinski, H., & Peters, B. (2012). Writing in style. In R. Miller (Ed.), *APA made easy: A new way of formatting.* New York, NY: Anchor Press.

Chapter in Book, English Translation, Four Authors

Anders, J., Matkovich, R. A., Swarinski, H., & Peters, B. (2014). Creating a new metaphor (R. Miller, Trans.). In B. Reynolds (Ed.), *Formatting for dummies* (pp. 3-56). Dallas, TX: Anchor Press.

Chapter in Book with Four Authors, Title with Proper Noun

Anders, J., Rossier, R. A., Swarinski, H., & Peters, B. (2014). Writing in style. In R. Miller (Ed.), *The life and times of J. Edgar Hoover.* New York, NY: Anchor Press.

Chapter in Book with Four Authors, Limited Circulation, Not Online

Anders, J., Matkovich, R. A., Swarinski, H., & Peters, B. (2014). Writing in style. In R. Miller (Ed.), *Creating a new metaphor.* (Available from Baker, 122 South Salem Street, Billings, MT. 59101)

Chapter in Book with Four Authors, Limited Circulation, From Database - include URL of database where chapter can be found

Anders, J., Matkovich, R. A., Swarinski, H., & Peters, B. (2014). Writing in style. In R. Miller (Ed.), *Creating a new metaphor*. Retrieved from http:// www.nameofonlinedatabaseurl.edu/onlinelimitedcirculation

Chapter in Book, English Translation, Four Authors

Anders, J., Matkovich, R. A., Swarinski, H., & Peters, B. (2014). Creating a new metaphor (R. Miller, Trans.). In B. Reynolds (Ed.), *Formatting for dummies* (pp. 3-56). Dallas, TX: Anchor Press.

Chapter in Book, English Translation, Four Authors, Reprinted from Another Source

Anders, J., Matkovich, R. A., Swarinski, H., & Peters, B. (2014). Creating a new metaphor (R. Miller, Trans.). In B. Reynolds (Ed.), *Formatting for dummies* (pp. 3-56). Dallas, TX: Anchor Press. (Reprinted from *Formatting for fun*, pp. 78-121, by B. B. Newby, Ed., 2000, Billings, MT: Newport Press).

Book with Four Authors, Ebook or Electronic Version

Anders, J., Matkovich, R. A., Swarinski, H., & Peters, B. (2014). *Writing with style*. Retrieved from http://www.apamadeasy.com/ebooks

Book with Four Authors, No Date, Ebook or Electronic Version

Anders, J., Matkovich, R. A., Swarinski, H., & Peters, B. (n.d.). *Writing with style*. Retrieved from http://www.apamadeasy.com/ebooks

Book with Four Authors, Ebook or Electronic Version, with DOI

Anders, J., Matkovich, R. A., Swarinski, H., & Peters, B. (2014). *Writing with style*. doi: 10.1234567890

Book with Four Authors, Ebook or Electronic Version, Republished Date - Use the latest date listed

Anders, J., Matkovich, R. A., Swarinski, H., & Peters, B. (2014). *Writing with style*. Retrieved from http://www.apamadeasy.com/ebooks

Book with Four Authors, Ebook or Electronic Version, with DOI - Republished Date - Use the latest date listed

Anders, J., Matkovich, R. A., Swarinski, H., & Peters, B. (2014). *Writing with style.* doi: 10.1234567890

Book with Four Authors, Ebook or Electronic Version, Edition Other Than First

Anders, J., Rossier, R. A., Swarinski, H., & Peters, B. (2012). *APA made easy* (4th ed.). Retrieved from http://www.apamadeasy.com/ebooks

Book with Four Authors, Ebook or Electronic Version, Revised Edition

Anders, J., Rossier, R. A., Swarinski, H., & Peters, B. (2012). *APA made easy* (Rev. ed.). Retrieved from http://www.apamadeasy.com/ebooks

Book with Four Authors, Ebook or Electronic Version, Title with Subtitle

Anders, J., Rossier, R. A., Swarinski, H., & Peters, B. (2012). *APA made easy: Writing with style.* Retrieved from http://www.apamadeasy.com/ebooks

Book with Four Authors, Ebook or Electronic Version, No Date, Title with Subtitle

Anders, J., Rossier, R. A., Swarinski, H., & Peters, B. (n.d.). *APA made easy: Writing with style.* Retrieved from http://www.apamadeasy.com/ebooks

Book with Four Authors, Ebook or Electronic Version, Title with Proper Noun

Anders, J., Rossier, R. A., Swarinski, H., & Peters, B. (2014). *The life and times of J. Edgar Hoover.* Retrieved from http://www.apamadeasy.com/ebooks

Book with Four Authors with Hyphenated Name

Anders, J.-R., Rossier, R. A., Swarinski, H., & Peters, B. (2014). *The life and times of J. Edgar Hoover.* New York, NY: Anchor Press.

Book with Four Authors, Ebook or Electronic Version, Title with Subtitle, Edition Other than First

Anders, J., Rossier, R. A., Swarinski, H., & Peters, B. (2014). *APA made easy: Writing with style* (4th ed.). Retrieved from http://www.apamadeasy.com/ebooks

Book with Four Authors, Ebook or Electronic Version, No Date, Title with Subtitle, Edition Other than First

Anders, J., Rossier, R. A., Swarinski, H., & Peters, B. (n.d.). *APA made easy: Writing with style* (4th ed.). Retrieved from http://www.apamadeasy.com/ebooks

Book with Four Authors, Ebook or Electronic Version, Title with Series

Anders, J., Rossier, R. A., Swarinski, H., & Peters, B. (2012). *APA made easy: Vol. 4. Writing with style.* Retrieved from http://www.apamadeasy.com/ebooks

Book with Four Authors, Electronic Version of Print Version from E-Reader (Kindle, Nook, etc.) - Type of Electronic version goes in brackets

Anders, J., Matkovich, R. A., Swarinski, H., & Peters, B. (2014). *APA made easy* [Kindle version]. Retrieved from http://www.youversustheworld.com/asp

Book with Four Authors, Electronic Version of Republished Print Book

Anders, J., Rossier, R. A., Swarinski, H., & Peters, B. (2014). Writing in style. In R. Miller (Ed.), *Problem solving while writing long books* (pp. 80-88). Retrieved from http://www.youversustheworld.com/urlexamples (Original work published 2001)

Book with Four Authors, Electronic Version of Republished Print Book, No Page Numbers Available

Anders, J., Rossier, R. A., Swarinski, H., & Peters, B. (2014). Writing in style. In R. Miller (Ed.), *Problem solving while writing long books.* Retrieved from http://www.youversustheworld.com/urlexamples

Chapter in Electronic Book/Ebook with Four Authors

Anders, J., Matkovich, R. A., Swarinski, H., & Peters, B. (2014). Writing in style. In R. Miller (Ed.), *Writing Fundamentals* (pp. 93-103). Retrieved from http://www.youversustheworld.com/chapterreferences

Chapter in Electronic Book/Ebook with Four Authors, with DOI

Anders, J., Matkovich, R. A., Swarinski, H., & Peters, B. (2014). Writing in style. In R. Miller (Ed.), *Writing Fundamentals* (pp. 93-103). doi:10.1234567890

Chapter in Electronic Book/Ebook with Four Authors, Title with Subtitle

Anders, J., Rossier, R. A., Swarinski, H., & Peters, B. (2012). Writing in style. In R. Miller (Ed.), *APA made easy: A new way of formatting*. Retrieved from http://www.youversustheworld.com/chapterreferences

Chapter in Electronic Book/Ebook with Four Authors, Republished Date - Use the latest date listed

Anders, J., Rossier, R. A., Swarinski, H., & Peters, B. (2012). Writing in style. In R. Miller (Ed.), *APA made easy*. Retrieved from http://www.youversustheworld.com/chapterreferences

Chapter in Electronic Book/Ebook with Four Authors, Title with Subtitle, Republished Date - Use the latest date listed

Anders, J., Rossier, R. A., Swarinski, H., & Peters, B. (2012). Writing in style. In R. Miller (Ed.), *APA made easy: Writing with style*. Retrieved from http://www.youversustheworld.com/chapterreferences

Chapter in Electronic Book/Ebook of Print Version from Republished Book with Four Authors, with Volume Number

Anders, J., Rossier, R. A., Swarinski, H., & Peters, B. (2014). Creating a new metaphor. In R. McClure (Ed.). *Writing with style* (Vol. 1, pp. 105-144). Retrieved from http://www.youversustheworld.com/chapterreference

Chapter in Electronic Book/Ebook, English Translation, Four Authors

Anders, J., Matkovich, R. A., Swarinski, H., & Peters, B. (2014). Creating a new metaphor (R. Miller, Trans.). In B. Reynolds (Ed.), *Formatting for dummies* (pp. 3-56). Retrieved from http://www.youversustheworld.com/chapterreferences

Chapter in Electronic Book/Ebook with Four Authors, Title with Proper Noun

Anders, J., Rossier, R. A., Swarinski, H., & Peters, B. (2014). Writing in style. In R. Miller (Ed.), *The life and times of J. Edgar Hoover*. Retrieved from http://www.youversustheworld.com/chapterreferences

Chapter in Electronic Book/Ebook with Four Authors, Limited Circulation, From Database - Include URL of database where chapter can be found

Anders, J., Matkovich, R. A., Swarinski, H., & Peters, B. (2014). Writing in style. In R. Miller (Ed.), *Creating a new metaphor.* Retrieved from http://www.nameofonlinedatabaseurl.edu/onlinelimitedcirculation

Chapter in Electronic Book/Ebook, English Translation, Four Authors

Anders, J., Matkovich, R. A., Swarinski, H., & Peters, B. (2014). Creating a new metaphor (R. Miller, Trans.). In B. Reynolds (Ed.), *Formatting for dummies* (pp. 3-56). Retrieved from http://www.youversustheworld.com/chapterreferences

Chapter in Electronic Book/Ebook, English Translation, Four Authors, Reprinted from Another Source

Anders, J., Matkovich, R. A., Swarinski, H., & Peters, B. (2014). Creating a new metaphor (R. Miller, Trans.). In B. Reynolds (Ed.), *Formatting for dummies* (pp. 3-56). Retrieved from http://www.youversustheworld.com/chapterreferences (Reprinted from *Formatting for fun*, pp. 78-121, by B. B. Newby, Ed., 2000, Billings, MT: Newport Press).

Chapter in Electronic Book/Ebook of Print Version with Four Authors (Kindle, Nook, etc.)

Anders, J., Rossier, R. A., Swarinski, H., & Peters, B. (2014). Creating a new metaphor. In R. McClure (Ed.). *Writing with style* [iBooks version]. Retrieved from http://www.ibooks.com/chapterreferences

Chapter in Electronic Book/Ebook of Print Version with Four Authors, with DOI

Anders, J., Rossier, R. A., Swarinski, H., & Peters, B. (2014). Creating a new metaphor. In R. McClure (Ed.). *Writing with style* [iBooks version]. doi: 10.1234567890

Reference Book with Four Authors - Only list Editor's Name

Anders, J., Rossier, R. A., Swarinski, H., & Peters, B. (Ed.). (2014). *References in obscurity.* Wauconda, IL: Anchor Press.

Entry in Reference Book with Four Authors

Anders, J., Rossier, R. A., Swarinski, H., & Peters, B. (2014). References in obscurity. In R. Miller (Ed.), *Getting references right* (3rd ed., Vol. 8). Wauconda, IL: Anchor Press.

Entry in Online Reference Book with Four Authors

Anders, J., Rossier, R. A., Swarinski, H., & Peters, B. (2014). References in obscurity. In R. Miller (Ed.), *Getting references right* (3rd ed., Vol. 8). Retrieved from http://www.youversustheworld.com/referencesbooks

Entry in Online Reference Book with Four Authors, with DOI

Anders, J., Rossier, R. A., Swarinski, H., & Peters, B. (2014). References in obscurity. In R. Miller (Ed.), *Getting references right* (3rd ed., Vol. 8). doi: 10.1234567890

Entry in Online Reference Book with Four Authors, with Page Numbers, with DOI

Anders, J., Rossier, R. A., Swarinski, H., & Peters, B. (2014). References in obscurity. In R. Miller (Ed.), *Getting references right* (pp. 251-298). doi:10.1234567890

Entry in Online Reference Book with Four Authors, Alternative Edition Example

Anders, J., Rossier, R. A., Swarinski, H., & Peters, B. (2014). References in obscurity. In R. Miller (Ed.), *Getting references right* (Spring 2008 ed.). Retrieved from http://www.youversustheworld.com/referencesbooks

Books with Five Authors

A Quick Overview : **Books with Five Authors**

Sample Reference Structure:

Last Name, First Initial., Second Last Name, First Initial., Third Last Name, Third First Initial., Fourth Last Name, Fourth First Initial., & Fifth Last Name, Fifth First Initial. (Date of Publication). *Title of publication.* City, State Initials of Publication: Publisher.

Example:

Beuregaard, S. P., Hume, D. A., Spinoza, B., Plantinga, A., & Craig, W. L. (2012). *APA made easy*. New York, NY: Anchor Press.

Electronic Sample

Last Name, First Initial., Second Last Name, First Initial., Third Last Name, Third First Initial., Fourth Last Name, Fourth First Initial., & Fifth Last Name, Fifth First Initial. (Date of Publication). *Title of publication.* Retrieved from http://nameofurl.com

Electronic Example

Beuregaard, S. P., Hume, D. A., Spinoza, B., Plantinga, A., & Craig, W. L. (2014). *Writing with style*. Retrieved from http://www.apamadeasy.com/ebooks

Sample In-Text Citations

For your first time citing a book with five authors, your in text citation should appear like this:
(Smith, Johnson, Hadden, Fuentes, & Zeigler, 2013)

For subsequent paragraph citation after the first
(Smith et al., 2013)

Every subsequent citation omits the year:
(Smith et al.)

Example #1: Paraphrase

There have been cases where people have compared Smith, Johnson, Hadden, Fuentes, and Zeigler (2012) to *APA Made Easy* because of the similarities in writing style.

Example #2: Paraphrase

Smith et al. (2012) have compared to APA formatting to MLA formatting.

Example #3: Second Instance of Paraphrase

Smith et al. have compared to APA formatting to MLA formatting.

Example #4: Direct Quote

The book on Fairy Tales was described as "a wonderful tale of hope and dreams" (Smith, Johnson, Haden, Fuentes, & Zeigler, 2012, p. 14).

Example #5: Direct Quote, Second Instance

The book on Fairy Tales was described as "a wonderful tale of hope and dreams" (Smith et al., 2012, p. 14).

Books with Five Authors

Book with Five Authors, Standard Date of Publication

Beuregaard, S. P., Hume, D. A., Spinoza, B., Plantinga, A., & Craig, W. L. (2012). *APA made easy*. New York, NY: Anchor Press.

Book with Five Authors, No Date

Beuregaard, S. P., Hume, D. A., Spinoza, B., Plantinga, A., & Craig, W. L. (n.d.). *APA made easy*. New York, NY: Anchor Press.

Book with Five Authors, Republished Date - Use the latest date listed

Beuregaard, S. P., Hume, D. A., Spinoza, B., Plantinga, A., & Craig, W. L. (2012). *APA made easy*. New York, NY: Anchor Press.

In Text Citation Example - Cite both the original published date and the date of the republished version:

(Beuregaard, Hume, Spinoza, Plantinga, & Craig, 2000/2012).

Book with Five Authors, Edition Other Than First

Beuregaard, S. P., Hume, D. A., Spinoza, B., Plantinga, A., & Craig, W. L. (2012). *APA made easy* (4th ed.). New York, NY: Anchor Press.

Book with Five Authors, Revised Edition

Beuregaard, S. P., Hume, D. A., Spinoza, B., Plantinga, A., & Craig, W. L. (2012). *APA made easy* (Rev. ed.). New York, NY: Anchor Press.

Book with Five Authors, Title with Subtitle

Beuregaard, S. P., Hume, D. A., Spinoza, B., Plantinga, A., & Craig, W. L. (2012). *APA made easy: Writing with style.* New York, NY: Anchor Press.

Book with Five Authors, No Date, Title with Subtitle

Beuregaard, S. P., Hume, D. A., Spinoza, B., Plantinga, A., & Craig, W. L. (n.d.). *APA made easy: Writing with style.* New York, NY: Anchor Press.

Book with Five Authors, Title with Proper Noun

Beuregaard, S. P., Hume, D. A., Spinoza, B., Plantinga, A., & Craig, W. L. (2014). *The life and times of J. Edgar Hoover.* New York, NY: Anchor Press.

Book with Five Authors with Hyphenated Name

Anders, J.-R., Hume, D. A., Spinoza, B., Plantinga, A., & Craig, W. L. (2014). *The life and times of J. Edgar Hoover.* New York, NY: Anchor Press.

Book with Five Authors, Title with Subtitle, Edition Other than First

Beuregaard, S. P., Hume, D. A., Spinoza, B., Plantinga, A., & Craig, W. L. (2014). *APA made easy: Writing with style* (4th ed.). New York, NY: Anchor Press.

Book with Five Authors, No Date, Title with Subtitle, Edition Other than First

Beuregaard, S. P., Hume, D. A., Spinoza, B., Plantinga, A., & Craig, W. L. (n.d.). *APA made easy: Writing with style* (4th ed.). New York, NY: Anchor Press.

Book with Five Authors, Title with Series

Beuregaard, S. P., Hume, D. A., Spinoza, B., Plantinga, A., & Craig, W. L. (2012). *APA made easy: Vol. 4. Writing with style.* New York, NY: Anchor Press.

Book with Five Authors, Limited Circulation, Not Online

Beuregaard, S. P., Hume, D. A., Spinoza, B., Plantinga, A., & Craig, W. L. (2014). *Creating a new metaphor.* (Available from Baker, 122 South Salem Street, Billings, MT. 59101)

Book with Five Authors, Limited Circulation, From Database

Beuregaard, S. P., Hume, D. A., Spinoza, B., Plantinga, A., & Craig, W. L. (2014). *Creating a new metaphor.* Retrieved from http://www.nameofonlinedatabaseurl.edu/onlinelimitedcirculation

Book with Five Authors, Monograph

Beuregaard, S. P., Hume, D. A., Spinoza, B., Plantinga, A., & Craig, W. L. (2014). *Creating a new metaphor* [Monograph]. Retrieved from http://www.nameofonlinedatabaseurl.edu/onlinelimitedcirculation

Book with Five Authors, No Date, Monograph

Beuregaard, S. P., Hume, D. A., Spinoza, B., Plantinga, A., & Craig, W. L. (n.d.). *Creating a new metaphor* [Monograph]. Retrieved from http://www.nameofonlinedatabaseurl.edu/onlinelimitedcirculation

Chapter in Book with Five Authors

Beuregaard, S. P., Hume, D. A., Spinoza, B., Plantinga, A., & Craig, W. L. (2014). Writing in style. In R. Miller (Ed.), *Writing Fundamentals* (pp. 93-103). New York, NY: Anchor Press.

Chapter in Book with Five Authors, Republished Date - Use the latest date listed

Beuregaard, S. P., Hume, D. A., Spinoza, B., Plantinga, A., & Craig, W. L. (2012). Writing in style. In R. Miller (Ed.), *APA made easy.* New York, NY: Anchor Press.

Chapter in Book with Five Authors, Title with Subtitle

Beuregaard, S. P., Hume, D. A., Spinoza, B., Plantinga, A., & Craig, W. L. (2012). Writing in style. In R. Miller (Ed.), *APA made easy: A new way of formatting.* New York, NY: Anchor Press.

Chapter in Book, English Translation, Five Authors

Beuregaard, S. P., Hume, D. A., Spinoza, B., Plantinga, A., & Craig, W. L. (2014). Creating a new metaphor (R. Miller, Trans.). In B. Reynolds (Ed.), *Formatting for dummies* (pp. 3-56). Dallas, TX: Anchor Press.

Chapter in Book with Five Authors, Title with Proper Noun

Beuregaard, S. P., Hume, D. A., Spinoza, B., Plantinga, A., & Craig, W. L. (2014). Writing in style. In R. Miller (Ed.), *The life and times of J. Edgar Hoover.* New York, NY: Anchor Press.

Chapter in Book with Five Authors, Limited Circulation, Not Online

Beuregaard, S. P., Hume, D. A., Spinoza, B., Plantinga, A., & Craig, W. L. (2014). Writing in style. In R. Miller (Ed.), *Creating a new metaphor.* (Available from Baker, 122 South Salem Street, Billings, MT. 59101)

Chapter in Book with Five Authors, Limited Circulation, From Database - include URL of database where chapter can be found

Beuregaard, S. P., Hume, D. A., Spinoza, B., Plantinga, A., & Craig, W. L. (2014). Writing in style. In R. Miller (Ed.), *Creating a new metaphor.* Retrieved from http://www.nameofonlinedatabaseurl.edu/onlinelimitedcirculation

Chapter in Book, English Translation, Five Authors

Beuregaard, S. P., Hume, D. A., Spinoza, B., Plantinga, A., & Craig, W. L. (2014). Creating a new metaphor (R. Miller, Trans.). In B. Reynolds (Ed.), *Formatting for dummies* (pp. 3-56). Dallas, TX: Anchor Press.

Chapter in Book, English Translation, Five Authors, Reprinted from Another Source

Beuregaard, S. P., Hume, D. A., Spinoza, B., Plantinga, A., & Craig, W. L. (2014). Creating a new metaphor (R. Miller, Trans.). In B. Reynolds (Ed.), *Formatting for dummies* (pp. 3-56). Dallas, TX: Anchor Press. (Reprinted from *Formatting for fun*, pp. 78-121, by B. B. Newby, Ed., 2000, Billings, MT: Newport Press).

Book with Five Authors, Ebook or Electronic Version

Beuregaard, S. P., Hume, D. A., Spinoza, B., Plantinga, A., & Craig, W. L. (2014). *Writing with style*. Retrieved from http://www.apamadeasy.com/ebooks

Book with Five Authors, No Date, Ebook or Electronic Version

Beuregaard, S. P., Hume, D. A., Spinoza, B., Plantinga, A., & Craig, W. L. (n.d.). *Writing with style*. Retrieved from http://www.apamadeasy.com/ebooks

Book with Five Authors, Ebook or Electronic Version, with DOI

Beuregaard, S. P., Hume, D. A., Spinoza, B., Plantinga, A., & Craig, W. L. (2014). *Writing with style*. doi:10.1234567890

Book with Five Authors, Ebook or Electronic Version, Republished Date - Use the latest date listed

Beuregaard, S. P., Hume, D. A., Spinoza, B., Plantinga, A., & Craig, W. L. (2014). *Writing with style*. Retrieved from http://www.apamadeasy.com/ebooks

Book with Five Authors, Ebook or Electronic Version, with DOI - Republished Date - Use the latest date listed

Beuregaard, S. P., Hume, D. A., Spinoza, B., Plantinga, A., & Craig, W. L. (2014). *Writing with style*. doi:10.1234567890

Book with Five Authors, Ebook or Electronic Version, Edition Other Than First

Beuregaard, S. P., Hume, D. A., Spinoza, B., Plantinga, A., & Craig, W. L. (2012). *APA made easy* (4th ed.). Retrieved from http://www.apamadeasy.com/ebooks

Book with Five Authors, Ebook or Electronic Version, Revised Edition

Beuregaard, S. P., Hume, D. A., Spinoza, B., Plantinga, A., & Craig, W. L. (2012). *APA made easy* (Rev. ed.). Retrieved from http://www.apamadeasy.com/ebooks

Book with Five Authors, Ebook or Electronic Version, Title with Subtitle

Beuregaard, S. P., Hume, D. A., Spinoza, B., Plantinga, A., & Craig, W. L. (2012). *APA made easy: Writing with style.* Retrieved from http://www.apamadeasy.com/ebooks

Book with Five Authors, Ebook or Electronic Version, No Date, Title with Subtitle

Beuregaard, S. P., Hume, D. A., Spinoza, B., Plantinga, A., & Craig, W. L. (n.d.). *APA made easy: Writing with style.* Retrieved from http://www.apamadeasy.com/ebooks

Book with Five Authors, Ebook or Electronic Version, Title with Proper Noun

Beuregaard, S. P., Hume, D. A., Spinoza, B., Plantinga, A., & Craig, W. L. (2014). *The life and times of J. Edgar Hoover.* Retrieved from http://www.apamadeasy.com/ebooks

Book with Five Authors, Ebook or Electronic Version, Title with Subtitle, Edition Other than First

Beuregaard, S. P., Hume, D. A., Spinoza, B., Plantinga, A., & Craig, W. L. (2014). *APA made easy: Writing with style* (4th ed.). Retrieved from http://www.apamadeasy.com/ebooks

Book with Five Authors, Ebook or Electronic Version, No Date, Title with Subtitle, Edition Other than First

Beuregaard, S. P., Hume, D. A., Spinoza, B., Plantinga, A., & Craig, W. L. (n.d.). *APA made easy: Writing with style* (4th ed.). Retrieved from http://www.apamadeasy.com/ebooks

Book with Five Authors, Ebook or Electronic Version, Title with Series

Beuregaard, S. P., Hume, D. A., Spinoza, B., Plantinga, A., & Craig, W. L. (2012). *APA made easy: Vol. 4. Writing with style.* Retrieved from http://www.apamadeasy.com/ebooks

Book with Five Authors, Electronic Version of Print Version from E-Reader (Kindle, Nook, etc.) - Type of Electronic version goes in brackets

Beuregaard, S. P., Hume, D. A., Spinoza, B., Plantinga, A., & Craig, W. L. (2014). *APA made easy* [Kindle version]. Retrieved from http://www.youversustheworld.com/asp

Book with Five Authors, Electronic Version of Republished Print Book

Beuregaard, S. P., Hume, D. A., Spinoza, B., Plantinga, A., & Craig, W. L. (2014). Writing in style. In R. Miller (Ed.), *Problem solving while writing long books* (pp. 80-88). Retrieved from http://www.youversustheworld.com/urlexamples (Original work published 2001)

Book with Five Authors, Electronic Version of Republished Print Book, No Page Numbers Available

Beuregaard, S. P., Hume, D. A., Spinoza, B., Plantinga, A., & Craig, W. L. (2014). Writing in style. In R. Miller (Ed.), *Problem solving while writing long books*. Retrieved from http://www.youversustheworld.com/urlexamples

Chapter in Electronic Book/Ebook with Five Authors

Beuregaard, S. P., Hume, D. A., Spinoza, B., Plantinga, A., & Craig, W. L. (2014). Writing in style. In R. Miller (Ed.), *Writing Fundamentals* (pp. 93-103). Retrieved from http://www.youversustheworld.com/chapterreferences

Chapter in Electronic Book/Ebook with Five Authors, with DOI

Beuregaard, S. P., Hume, D. A., Spinoza, B., Plantinga, A., & Craig, W. L. (2014). Writing in style. In R. Miller (Ed.), *Writing Fundamentals* (pp. 93-103). doi: 10.1234567890

Chapter in Electronic Book/Ebook with Five Authors, Title with Subtitle

Beuregaard, S. P., Hume, D. A., Spinoza, B., Plantinga, A., & Craig, W. L. (2012). Writing in style. In R. Miller (Ed.), *APA made easy: A new way of formatting*. Retrieved from http://www.youversustheworld.com/chapterreferences

Chapter in Electronic Book/Ebook with Five Authors, Republished Date - Use the latest date listed

Beuregaard, S. P., Hume, D. A., Spinoza, B., Plantinga, A., & Craig, W. L. (2012). Writing in style. In R. Miller (Ed.), *APA made easy*. Retrieved from http://www.youversustheworld.com/chapterreferences

Chapter in Electronic Book/Ebook with Five Authors, Title with Subtitle, Republished Date - Use the latest date listed

Beuregaard, S. P., Hume, D. A., Spinoza, B., Plantinga, A., & Craig, W. L. (2012). Writing in style. In R. Miller (Ed.), *APA made easy: Writing with style.* Retrieved from http://www.youversustheworld.com/chapterreferences

Chapter in Electronic Book/Ebook of Print Version from Republished Book with Five Authors, with Volume Number

Beuregaard, S. P., Hume, D. A., Spinoza, B., Plantinga, A., & Craig, W. L. (2014). Creating a new metaphor. In R. McClure (Ed.). *Writing with style* (Vol. 1, pp. 105-144). Retrieved from http://www.youversustheworld.com/chapterreference

Chapter in Electronic Book/Ebook, English Translation, Five Authors

Beuregaard, S. P., Hume, D. A., Spinoza, B., Plantinga, A., & Craig, W. L. (2014). Creating a new metaphor (R. Miller, Trans.). In B. Reynolds (Ed.), *Formatting for dummies* (pp. 3-56). Retrieved from http://www.youversustheworld.com/chapterreferences

Chapter in Electronic Book/Ebook with Five Authors, Title with Proper Noun

Beuregaard, S. P., Hume, D. A., Spinoza, B., Plantinga, A., & Craig, W. L. (2014). Writing in style. In R. Miller (Ed.), *The life and times of J. Edgar Hoover.* Retrieved from http://www.youversustheworld.com/chapterreferences

Chapter in Electronic Book/Ebook with Five Authors, Limited Circulation, From Database - Include URL of database where chapter can be found

Beuregaard, S. P., Hume, D. A., Spinoza, B., Plantinga, A., & Craig, W. L. (2014). Writing in style. In R. Miller (Ed.), *Creating a new metaphor.* Retrieved from http://www.nameofonlinedatabaseurl.edu/onlinelimitedcirculation

Chapter in Electronic Book/Ebook, English Translation, Five Authors

Beuregaard, S. P., Hume, D. A., Spinoza, B., Plantinga, A., & Craig, W. L. (2014). Creating a new metaphor (R. Miller, Trans.). In B. Reynolds (Ed.), *Formatting for dummies* (pp. 3-56). Retrieved from http://www.youversustheworld.com/chapterreferences

Chapter in Electronic Book/Ebook, English Translation, Five Authors, Reprinted from Another Source

Beuregaard, S. P., Hume, D. A., Spinoza, B., Plantinga, A., & Craig, W. L. (2014). Creating a new metaphor (R. Miller, Trans.). In B. Reynolds (Ed.), *Formatting for dummies* (pp. 3-56). Retrieved from http://www.youversustheworld.com/chapterreferences (Reprinted from *Formatting for fun*, pp. 78-121, by B. B. Newby, Ed., 2000, Billings, MT: Newport Press).

Chapter in Electronic Book/Ebook of Print Version with Five Authors (Kindle, Nook, etc.)

Beuregaard, S. P., Hume, D. A., Spinoza, B., Plantinga, A., & Craig, W. L. (2014). Creating a new metaphor. In R. McClure (Ed.). *Writing with style* [iBooks version]. Retrieved from http://www.ibooks.com/chapterreferences

Chapter in Electronic Book/Ebook of Print Version with Five Authors, with DOI

Beuregaard, S. P., Hume, D. A., Spinoza, B., Plantinga, A., & Craig, W. L. (2014). Creating a new metaphor. In R. McClure (Ed.). *Writing with style* [iBooks version]. doi: 10.1234567890

Reference Book with Five Authors - Only list Editor's Name

Beuregaard, S. P., Hume, D. A., Spinoza, B., Plantinga, A., & Craig, W. L. (Ed.). (2014). *References in obscurity*. Wauconda, IL: Anchor Press.

Entry in Reference Book with Five Authors

Beuregaard, S. P., Hume, D. A., Spinoza, B., Plantinga, A., & Craig, W. L. (2014). References in obscurity. In R. Miller (Ed.), *Getting references right* (3rd ed., Vol. 8). Wauconda, IL: Anchor Press.

Entry in Online Reference Book with Five Authors

Beuregaard, S. P., Hume, D. A., Spinoza, B., Plantinga, A., & Craig, W. L. (2014). References in obscurity. In R. Miller (Ed.), *Getting references right* (3rd ed., Vol. 8). Retrieved from http://www.youversustheworld.com/referencesbooks

Entry in Online Reference Book with Five Authors, with DOI

Beuregaard, S. P., Hume, D. A., Spinoza, B., Plantinga, A., & Craig, W. L. (2014). References in obscurity. In R. Miller (Ed.), *Getting references right* (3rd ed., Vol. 8). doi: 10.1234567890

Entry in Online Reference Book with Five Authors, with Page Numbers, with DOI

Beuregaard, S. P., Hume, D. A., Spinoza, B., Plantinga, A., & Craig, W. L. (2014). References in obscurity. In R. Miller (Ed.), *Getting references right* (pp. 251-298). doi:10.1234567890

Entry in Online Reference Book with Five Authors, Alternative Edition Example

Beuregaard, S. P., Hume, D. A., Spinoza, B., Plantinga, A., & Craig, W. L. (2014). References in obscurity. In R. Miller (Ed.), *Getting references right* (Spring 2008 ed.). Retrieved from http://www.youversustheworld.com/referencesbooks

Books with Six Authors

A Quick Overview : **Books with Six Authors**

Sample Reference Structure:

Last Name, First Initial., Second Last Name, First Initial., Third Last Name, Third First Initial., Fifth Last Name, Fifth First Initial., & Sixth Last Name, Sixth First Initial. (Date of Publication). *Title of publication.* City, State Initials of Publication: Publisher.

Example:

Creston, J. P., Anders, R. F., Wilson, D. A., Peters, B. O., Roberts, M. A., & Nehman, T. (2012). *APA made easy.* New York, NY: Anchor Press.

Electronic Sample

Last Name, First Initial., Second Last Name, First Initial., Third Last Name, Third First Initial., Fifth Last Name, Fifth First Initial., & Sixth Last Name, Sixth First Initial. (Date of Publication). *Title of publication.* Retrieved from http://nameofurl.com

Electronic Example

Creston, J. P., Anders, R. F., Wilson, D. A., Peters, B. O., Roberts, M. A., & Nehman, T. (2014). *Writing with style.* Retrieved from http://www.apamadeasy.com/ebooks

Sample In-Text Citations

Example #1: Paraphrase

According to Anders et al. (2012), writing in APA format can be easy.

Example #2: Paraphrase

With so many resources available, writing in APA format can be easy (Anders et al., 2012).

Example #3: Direct Quote

Anders et al. (2012) stated, "Writing in APA format can be easy" (p. 6).

Example #4: Direct Quote
With so many resources available, writing in APA format can be easy (Anders et al., 2012, p. 6).

Books with Six Authors

Book with Six Authors, Standard Date of Publication

Creston, J. P., Anders, R. F., Wilson, D. A., Peters, B. O., Roberts, M. A., & Nehman, T. (2012). *APA made easy.* New York, NY: Anchor Press.

Book with Six Authors, No Date

Creston, J. P., Anders, R. F., Wilson, D. A., Peters, B. O., Roberts, M. A., & Nehman, T. (n.d.). *APA made easy.* New York, NY: Anchor Press.

Book with Six Authors, Republished Date - Use the latest date listed

Creston, J. P., Anders, R. F., Wilson, D. A., Peters, B. O., Roberts, M. A., & Nehman, T. (2012). *APA made easy.* New York, NY: Anchor Press.

In Text Citation Example - Cite both the original published date and the date of the republished version:
(Creston et al., 2000/2012).

Book with Six Authors, Edition Other Than First

Creston, J. P., Anders, R. F., Wilson, D. A., Peters, B. O., Roberts, M. A., & Nehman, T. (2012). *APA made easy* (4th ed.). New York, NY: Anchor Press.

Book with Six Authors, Revised Edition

Creston, J. P., Anders, R. F., Wilson, D. A., Peters, B. O., Roberts, M. A., & Nehman, T. (2012). *APA made easy* (Rev. ed.). New York, NY: Anchor Press.

Book with Six Authors, Title with Subtitle

Creston, J. P., Anders, R. F., Wilson, D. A., Peters, B. O., Roberts, M. A., & Nehman, T. (2012). *APA made easy: Writing with style.* New York, NY: Anchor Press.

Book with Six Authors, No Date, Title with Subtitle

Creston, J. P., Anders, R. F., Wilson, D. A., Peters, B. O., Roberts, M. A., & Nehman, T. (n.d.). *APA made easy: Writing with style.* New York, NY: Anchor Press.

Book with Six Authors, Title with Proper Noun

Creston, J. P., Anders, R. F., Wilson, D. A., Peters, B. O., Roberts, M. A., & Nehman, T. (2014). *The life and times of J. Edgar Hoover.* New York, NY: Anchor Press.

Book with Six Authors with Hyphenated Name

Anders, J.-R., Anders, R. F., Wilson, D. A., Peters, B. O., Roberts, M. A., & Nehman, T. (2014). *The life and times of J. Edgar Hoover.* New York, NY: Anchor Press.

Book with Six Authors, Title with Subtitle, Edition Other than First

Creston, J. P., Anders, R. F., Wilson, D. A., Peters, B. O., Roberts, M. A., & Nehman, T. (2014). *APA made easy: Writing with style* (4th ed.). New York, NY: Anchor Press.

Book with Six Authors, No Date, Title with Subtitle, Edition Other than First

Creston, J. P., Anders, R. F., Wilson, D. A., Peters, B. O., Roberts, M. A., & Nehman, T. (n.d.). *APA made easy: Writing with style* (4th ed.). New York, NY: Anchor Press.

Book with Six Authors, Title with Series

Creston, J. P., Anders, R. F., Wilson, D. A., Peters, B. O., Roberts, M. A., & Nehman, T. (2012). *APA made easy: Vol. 4. Writing with style.* New York, NY: Anchor Press.

Book with Six Authors, Limited Circulation, Not Online

Creston, J. P., Anders, R. F., Wilson, D. A., Peters, B. O., Roberts, M. A., & Nehman, T. (2014). *Creating a new metaphor.* (Available from Baker, 122 South Salem Street, Billings, MT. 59101)

Book with Six Authors, Limited Circulation, From Database

Creston, J. P., Anders, R. F., Wilson, D. A., Peters, B. O., Roberts, M. A., & Nehman, T. (2014). *Creating a new metaphor.* Retrieved from http://www.nameofonlinedatabaseurl.edu/onlinelimitedcirculation

Book with Six Authors, Monograph

Creston, J. P., Anders, R. F., Wilson, D. A., Peters, B. O., Roberts, M. A., & Nehman, T. (2014). *Creating a new metaphor* [Monograph]. Retrieved from http://www.nameofonlinedatabaseurl.edu/onlinelimitedcirculation

Book with Six Authors, No Date, Monograph

Creston, J. P., Anders, R. F., Wilson, D. A., Peters, B. O., Roberts, M. A., & Nehman, T. (n.d.). *Creating a new metaphor* [Monograph]. Retrieved from http://www.nameofonlinedatabaseurl.edu/onlinelimitedcirculation

Chapter in Book with Six Authors

Creston, J. P., Anders, R. F., Wilson, D. A., Peters, B. O., Roberts, M. A., & Nehman, T. (2014). Writing in style. In R. Miller (Ed.), *Writing Fundamentals* (pp. 93-103). New York, NY: Anchor Press.

Chapter in Book with Six Authors, Republished Date - Use the latest date listed

Creston, J. P., Anders, R. F., Wilson, D. A., Peters, B. O., Roberts, M. A., & Nehman, T. (2012). Writing in style. In R. Miller (Ed.), *APA made easy*. New York, NY: Anchor Press.

Chapter in Book with Six Authors, Title with Subtitle

Creston, J. P., Anders, R. F., Wilson, D. A., Peters, B. O., Roberts, M. A., & Nehman, T. (2012). Writing in style. In R. Miller (Ed.), *APA made easy: A new way of formatting*. New York, NY: Anchor Press.

Chapter in Book, English Translation, Six Authors

Creston, J. P., Anders, R. F., Wilson, D. A., Peters, B. O., Roberts, M. A., & Nehman, T. (2012). Creating a new metaphor (R. Miller, Trans.). In B. Reynolds (Ed.), *Formatting for dummies* (pp. 3-56). Dallas, TX: Anchor Press.

Chapter in Book with Six Authors, Title with Proper Noun

Creston, J. P., Anders, R. F., Wilson, D. A., Peters, B. O., Roberts, M. A., & Nehman, T. (2014). Writing in style. In R. Miller (Ed.), *The life and times of J. Edgar Hoover*. New York, NY: Anchor Press.

Chapter in Book with Six Authors, Limited Circulation, Not Online

Creston, J. P., Anders, R. F., Wilson, D. A., Peters, B. O., Roberts, M. A., & Nehman, T. (2014). Writing in style. In R. Miller (Ed.), *Creating a new metaphor.* (Available from Baker, 122 South Salem Street, Billings, MT. 59101)

Chapter in Book with Six Authors, Limited Circulation, From Database - include URL of database where chapter can be found

Creston, J. P., Anders, R. F., Wilson, D. A., Peters, B. O., Roberts, M. A., & Nehman, T. (2014). Writing in style. In R. Miller (Ed.), *Creating a new metaphor.* Retrieved from http://www.nameofonlinedatabaseurl.edu/onlinelimitedcirculation

Chapter in Book, English Translation, Six Authors, Reprinted from Another Source

Creston, J. P., Anders, R. F., Wilson, D. A., Peters, B. O., Roberts, M. A., & Nehman, T. (2014). Creating a new metaphor (R. Miller, Trans.). In B. Reynolds (Ed.), *Formatting for dummies* (pp. 3-56). Dallas, TX: Anchor Press. (Reprinted from *Formatting for fun*, pp. 78-121, by B. B. Newby, Ed., 2000, Billings, MT: Newport Press).

Book with Six Authors, Ebook or Electronic Version

Creston, J. P., Anders, R. F., Wilson, D. A., Peters, B. O., Roberts, M. A., & Nehman, T. (2014). *Writing with style.* Retrieved from http://www.apamadeasy.com/ebooks

Book with Six Authors, No Date, Ebook or Electronic Version

Creston, J. P., Anders, R. F., Wilson, D. A., Peters, B. O., Roberts, M. A., & Nehman, T. (2014). *Writing with style.* Retrieved from http://www.apamadeasy.com/ebooks

Book with Six Authors, Ebook or Electronic Version, with DOI

Creston, J. P., Anders, R. F., Wilson, D. A., Peters, B. O., Roberts, M. A., & Nehman, T. (2012). *Writing with style.* doi:10.1234567890

Book with Six Authors, Ebook or Electronic Version, Republished Date - Use the latest date listed

Creston, J. P., Anders, R. F., Wilson, D. A., Peters, B. O., Roberts, M. A., & Nehman, T. (2012). *Writing with style.* Retrieved from http://www.apamadeasy.com/ebooks

Book with Six Authors, Ebook or Electronic Version, with DOI - Republished Date - Use the latest date listed

Creston, J. P., Anders, R. F., Wilson, D. A., Peters, B. O., Roberts, M. A., & Nehman, T. (2012). *Writing with style.* doi:10.1234567890

Book with Six Authors, Ebook or Electronic Version, Edition Other Than First

Creston, J. P., Anders, R. F., Wilson, D. A., Peters, B. O., Roberts, M. A., & Nehman, T. (2012). *APA made easy* (4th ed.). Retrieved from http://www.apamadeasy.com/ebooks

Book with Six Authors, Ebook or Electronic Version, Revised Edition

Creston, J. P., Anders, R. F., Wilson, D. A., Peters, B. O., Roberts, M. A., & Nehman, T. (2012). *APA made easy* (Rev. ed.). Retrieved from http://www.apamadeasy.com/ebooks

Book with Six Authors, Ebook or Electronic Version, Title with Subtitle

Creston, J. P., Anders, R. F., Wilson, D. A., Peters, B. O., Roberts, M. A., & Nehman, T. (2012). *APA made easy: Writing with style.* Retrieved from http://www.apamadeasy.com/ebooks

Book with Six Authors, Ebook or Electronic Version, No Date, Title with Subtitle

Creston, J. P., Anders, R. F., Wilson, D. A., Peters, B. O., Roberts, M. A., & Nehman, T. (n.d.). *APA made easy: Writing with style.* Retrieved from http://www.apamadeasy.com/ebooks

Book with Six Authors, Ebook or Electronic Version, Title with Proper Noun

Creston, J. P., Anders, R. F., Wilson, D. A., Peters, B. O., Roberts, M. A., & Nehman, T. (2014). *The life and times of J. Edgar Hoover.* Retrieved from http://www.apamadeasy.com/ebooks

Book with Six Authors, Ebook or Electronic Version, Title with Subtitle, Edition Other than First

Creston, J. P., Anders, R. F., Wilson, D. A., Peters, B. O., Roberts, M. A., & Nehman, T. (2014). *APA made easy: Writing with style* (4th ed.). Retrieved from http://www.apamadeasy.com/ebooks

Book with Six Authors, Ebook or Electronic Version, No Date, Title with Subtitle, Edition Other than First

Creston, J. P., Anders, R. F., Wilson, D. A., Peters, B. O., Roberts, M. A., & Nehman, T. (n.d.). *APA made easy: Writing with style* (4th ed.). Retrieved from http://www.apamadeasy.com/ebooks

Book with Six Authors, Ebook or Electronic Version, Title with Series

Creston, J. P., Anders, R. F., Wilson, D. A., Peters, B. O., Roberts, M. A., & Nehman, T. (2012). *APA made easy: Vol. 4. Writing with style.* Retrieved from http://www.apamadeasy.com/ebooks

Book with Six Authors, Electronic Version of Print Version from E-Reader (Kindle, Nook, etc.) - Type of Electronic version goes in brackets

Creston, J. P., Anders, R. F., Wilson, D. A., Peters, B. O., Roberts, M. A., & Nehman, T. (2014). *APA made easy* [Kindle version]. Retrieved from http://www.youversustheworld.com/asp

Book with Six Authors, Electronic Version of Republished Print Book

Creston, J. P., Anders, R. F., Wilson, D. A., Peters, B. O., Roberts, M. A., & Nehman, T. (2014). Writing in style. In R. Miller (Ed.), *Problem solving while writing long books* (pp. 80-88). Retrieved from http://www.youversustheworld.com/urlexamples (Original work published 2001)

Book with Six Authors, Electronic Version of Republished Print Book, No Page Numbers Available

Creston, J. P., Anders, R. F., Wilson, D. A., Peters, B. O., Roberts, M. A., & Nehman, T. (2014). Writing in style. In R. Miller (Ed.), *Problem solving while writing long books.* Retrieved from http://www.youversustheworld.com/urlexamples

Chapter in Electronic Book/Ebook with Six Authors

Creston, J. P., Anders, R. F., Wilson, D. A., Peters, B. O., Roberts, M. A., & Nehman, T. (2014). Writing in style. In R. Miller (Ed.), *Writing Fundamentals* (pp. 93-103). Retrieved from http://www.youversustheworld.com/chapterreferences

Chapter in Electronic Book/Ebook with Six Authors, with DOI

Creston, J. P., Anders, R. F., Wilson, D. A., Peters, B. O., Roberts, M. A., & Nehman, T. (2014). Writing in style. In R. Miller (Ed.), *Writing Fundamentals* (pp. 93-103). doi: 10.1234567890

Chapter in Electronic Book/Ebook with Six Authors, Title with Subtitle

Creston, J. P., Anders, R. F., Wilson, D. A., Peters, B. O., Roberts, M. A., & Nehman, T. (2012). Writing in style. In R. Miller (Ed.), *APA made easy: A new way of formatting.* Retrieved from http://www.youversustheworld.com/chapterreferences

Chapter in Electronic Book/Ebook with Six Authors, Republished Date - Use the latest date listed

Creston, J. P., Anders, R. F., Wilson, D. A., Peters, B. O., Roberts, M. A., & Nehman, T. (2012). Writing in style. In R. Miller (Ed.), *APA made easy.* Retrieved from http://www.youversustheworld.com/chapterreferences

Chapter in Electronic Book/Ebook with Six Authors, Title with Subtitle, Republished Date - Use the latest date listed

Creston, J. P., Anders, R. F., Wilson, D. A., Peters, B. O., Roberts, M. A., & Nehman, T. (2012). Writing in style. In R. Miller (Ed.), *APA made easy: Writing with style.* Retrieved from http://www.youversustheworld.com/chapterreferences

Chapter in Electronic Book/Ebook of Print Version from Republished Book with Six Authors, with Volume Number

Creston, J. P., Anders, R. F., Wilson, D. A., Peters, B. O., Roberts, M. A., & Nehman, T. (2014). Creating a new metaphor. In R. McClure (Ed.). *Writing with style* (Vol. 1, pp. 105-144). Retrieved from http://www.youversustheworld.com/chapterreference

Chapter in Electronic Book/Ebook, English Translation, Six Authors

Creston, J. P., Anders, R. F., Wilson, D. A., Peters, B. O., Roberts, M. A., & Nehman, T. (2014). Creating a new metaphor (R. Miller, Trans.). In B. Reynolds (Ed.), *Formatting for dummies* (pp. 3-56). Retrieved from http://www.youversustheworld.com/chapterreferences

Chapter in Electronic Book/Ebook with Six Authors, Title with Proper Noun

Creston, J. P., Anders, R. F., Wilson, D. A., Peters, B. O., Roberts, M. A., & Nehman, T. (2014). Writing in style. In R. Miller (Ed.), *The life and times of J. Edgar Hoover.* Retrieved from http://www.youversustheworld.com/chapterreferences

Chapter in Electronic Book/Ebook with Six Authors, Limited Circulation, From Database - Include URL of database where chapter can be found

Creston, J. P., Anders, R. F., Wilson, D. A., Peters, B. O., Roberts, M. A., & Nehman, T. (2014). Writing in style. In R. Miller (Ed.), *Creating a new metaphor.* Retrieved from http://www.nameofonlinedatabaseurl.edu/onlinelimitedcirculation

Chapter in Electronic Book/Ebook, English Translation, Six Authors

Creston, J. P., Anders, R. F., Wilson, D. A., Peters, B. O., Roberts, M. A., & Nehman, T. (2014). Creating a new metaphor (R. Miller, Trans.). In B. Reynolds (Ed.), *Formatting for dummies* (pp. 3-56). Retrieved from http://www.youversustheworld.com/chapterreferences

Chapter in Electronic Book/Ebook, English Translation, Six Authors, Reprinted from Another Source

Creston, J. P., Anders, R. F., Wilson, D. A., Peters, B. O., Roberts, M. A., & Nehman, T. (2012). Creating a new metaphor (R. Miller, Trans.). In B. Reynolds (Ed.), *Formatting for dummies* (pp. 3-56). Retrieved from http://www.youversustheworld.com/chapterreferences (Reprinted from *Formatting for fun*, pp. 78-121, by B. B. Newby, Ed., 2000, Billings, MT: Newport Press).

Chapter in Electronic Book/Ebook of Print Version with Six Authors (Kindle, Nook, etc.)

Creston, J. P., Anders, R. F., Wilson, D. A., Peters, B. O., Roberts, M. A., & Nehman, T. (2014). Creating a new metaphor. In R. McClure (Ed.). *Writing with style* [iBooks version]. Retrieved from http://www.ibooks.com/chapterreferences

Chapter in Electronic Book/Ebook of Print Version with Six Authors, with DOI

Creston, J. P., Anders, R. F., Wilson, D. A., Peters, B. O., Roberts, M. A., & Nehman, T. (2014). Creating a new metaphor. In R. McClure (Ed.). *Writing with style* [iBooks version]. doi:10.1234567890

Reference Book with Six Authors - Only list Editor's Name

Creston, J. P., Anders, R. F., Wilson, D. A., Peters, B. O., Roberts, M. A., & Nehman, T. (Ed.). (2014). *References in obscurity*. Wauconda, IL: Anchor Press.

Entry in Reference Book with Six Authors

Creston, J. P., Anders, R. F., Wilson, D. A., Peters, B. O., Roberts, M. A., & Nehman, T. (2014). References in obscurity. In R. Miller (Ed.), *Getting references right* (3rd ed., Vol. 8). Wauconda, IL: Anchor Press.

Entry in Online Reference Book with Six Authors

Creston, J. P., Anders, R. F., Wilson, D. A., Peters, B. O., Roberts, M. A., & Nehman, T. (2014). References in obscurity. In R. Miller (Ed.), *Getting references right* (3rd ed., Vol. 8). Retrieved from http://www.youversustheworld.com/referencesbooks

Entry in Online Reference Book with Six Authors, with DOI

Creston, J. P., Anders, R. F., Wilson, D. A., Peters, B. O., Roberts, M. A., & Nehman, T. (2014). References in obscurity. In R. Miller (Ed.), *Getting references right* (3rd ed., Vol. 8). doi:10.1234567890

Entry in Online Reference Book with Six Authors, with Page Numbers, with DOI

Creston, J. P., Anders, R. F., Wilson, D. A., Peters, B. O., Roberts, M. A., & Nehman, T. (2014). References in obscurity. In R. Miller (Ed.), *Getting references right* (pp. 251-298). doi:10.1234567890

Entry in Online Reference Book with Six Authors, Alternative Edition Example

Creston, J. P., Anders, R. F., Wilson, D. A., Peters, B. O., Roberts, M. A., & Nehman, T. (2014). References in obscurity. In R. Miller (Ed.), *Getting references right* (Spring 2008 ed.). Retrieved from http://www.youversustheworld.com/referencesbooks

Books with Seven Authors

A Quick Overview : **Books with Seven Authors**

Sample Reference Structure:

Last Name, First Initial., Second Last Name, First Initial., Third Last Name, Third First Initial., Fourth Last Name, Fouth First Initial., Fifth Last Name, Fifth First Initial., Sixth Last Name, Sixth First Initial., & Seventh Last Name, Seventh First Initial. (Date of Publication). *Title of publication.* City, State Initials of Publication: Publisher.

Example:

Whitters, M. J., Crossen, J. D., Matthews, P., Homes, R., Keller, J. R., Moreland, J. P., & Lorenzen, S. (2012). *APA made easy.* New York, NY: Anchor Press.

Electronic Sample

Last Name, First Initial., Second Last Name, First Initial., Third Last Name, Third First Initial., Fourth Last Name, Fouth First Initial., Fifth Last Name, Fifth First Initial., Sixth Last Name, Sixth First Initial., & Seventh Last Name, Seventh First Initial. (Date of Publication). *Title of publication.* Retrieved from http://nameofurl.com

Electronic Example

Whitters, M. J., Crossen, J. D., Matthews, P., Homes, R., Keller, J. R., Moreland, J. P., & Lorenzen, S. (2014). *Writing with style.* Retrieved from http://www.apamadeasy.com/ebooks

Sample In-Text Citations

Example #1: Paraphrase

According to Anders et al. (2012), writing in APA format can be easy.

Example #2: Paraphrase

With so many resources available, writing in APA format can be easy (Anders et al., 2012).

Example #3: Direct Quote

Anders et al. (2012) stated, "Writing in APA format can be easy" (p. 8).

Example #4: Direct Quote

With so many resources available, writing in APA format can be easy (Anders et al., 2012, p. 8).

Books with Seven Authors

Book with Seven Authors, Standard Date of Publication

Whitters, M. J., Crossen, J. D., Matthews, P., Homes, R., Keller, J. R., Moreland, J. P., & Lorenzen, S. (2012). *APA made easy.* New York, NY: Anchor Press.

Book with Seven Authors, No Date

Whitters, M. J., Crossen, J. D., Matthews, P., Homes, R., Keller, J. R., Moreland, J. P., & Lorenzen, S. (n.d.). *APA made easy.* New York, NY: Anchor Press.

Book with Seven Authors, Republished Date - Use the latest date listed

Whitters, M. J., Crossen, J. D., Matthews, P., Homes, R., Keller, J. R., Moreland, J. P., & Lorenzen, S. (2012). *APA made easy.* New York, NY: Anchor Press.

In Text Citation Example - Cite both the original published date and the date of the republished version:

(Whitters et al., 2000/2012).

Book with Seven Authors, Edition Other Than First

Whitters, M. J., Crossen, J. D., Matthews, P., Homes, R., Keller, J. R., Moreland, J. P., & Lorenzen, S. (2012). *APA made easy* (4th ed.). New York, NY: Anchor Press.

Book with Seven Authors, Revised Edition

Whitters, M. J., Crossen, J. D., Matthews, P., Homes, R., Keller, J. R., Moreland, J. P., & Lorenzen, S. (2012). *APA made easy* (Rev. ed.). New York, NY: Anchor Press.

Book with Seven Authors, Title with Subtitle

Whitters, M. J., Crossen, J. D., Matthews, P., Homes, R., Keller, J. R., Moreland, J. P., & Lorenzen, S. (2012). *APA made easy: Writing with style.* New York, NY: Anchor Press.

Book with Seven Authors, No Date, Title with Subtitle

Whitters, M. J., Crossen, J. D., Matthews, P., Homes, R., Keller, J. R., Moreland, J. P., & Lorenzen, S. (n.d.). *APA made easy: Writing with style.* New York, NY: Anchor Press.

Book with Seven Authors, Title with Proper Noun

Whitters, M. J., Crossen, J. D., Matthews, P., Homes, R., Keller, J. R., Moreland, J. P., & Lorenzen, S. (2014). *The life and times of J. Edgar Hoover.* New York, NY: Anchor Press.

Book with Seven Authors with Hyphenated Name

Anders, J.-R., Crossen, J. D., Matthews, P., Homes, R., Keller, J. R., Moreland, J. P., & Lorenzen, S. (2014). *The life and times of J. Edgar Hoover.* New York, NY: Anchor Press.

Book with Seven Authors, Title with Subtitle, Edition Other than First

Whitters, M. J., Crossen, J. D., Matthews, P., Homes, R., Keller, J. R., Moreland, J. P., & Lorenzen, S. (2014). *APA made easy: Writing with style* (4th ed.). New York, NY: Anchor Press.

Book with Seven Authors, No Date, Title with Subtitle, Edition Other than First

Whitters, M. J., Crossen, J. D., Matthews, P., Homes, R., Keller, J. R., Moreland, J. P., & Lorenzen, S. (n.d.). *APA made easy: Writing with style* (4th ed.). New York, NY: Anchor Press.

Book with Seven Authors, Title with Series

Whitters, M. J., Crossen, J. D., Matthews, P., Homes, R., Keller, J. R., Moreland, J. P., & Lorenzen, S. (2012). *APA made easy: Vol. 4. Writing with style.* New York, NY: Anchor Press.

Book with Seven Authors, Limited Circulation, Not Online

Whitters, M. J., Crossen, J. D., Matthews, P., Homes, R., Keller, J. R., Moreland, J. P., & Lorenzen, S. (2014). *Creating a new metaphor.* (Available from Baker, 122 South Salem Street, Billings, MT. 59101)

Book with Seven Authors, Limited Circulation, From Database

Whitters, M. J., Crossen, J. D., Matthews, P., Homes, R., Keller, J. R., Moreland, J. P., & Lorenzen, S. (2014). *Creating a new metaphor.* Retrieved from http://www.nameofonlinedatabaseurl.edu/onlinelimitedcirculation

Book with Seven Authors, Monograph

Whitters, M. J., Crossen, J. D., Matthews, P., Homes, R., Keller, J. R., Moreland, J. P., & Lorenzen, S. (2014). *Creating a new metaphor* [Monograph]. Retrieved from http://www.nameofonlinedatabaseurl.edu/onlinelimitedcirculation

Book with Seven Authors, No Date, Monograph

Whitters, M. J., Crossen, J. D., Matthews, P., Homes, R., Keller, J. R., Moreland, J. P., & Lorenzen, S. (n.d.). *Creating a new metaphor* [Monograph]. Retrieved from http://www.nameofonlinedatabaseurl.edu/onlinelimitedcirculation

Chapter in Book with Seven Authors

Whitters, M. J., Crossen, J. D., Matthews, P., Homes, R., Keller, J. R., Moreland, J. P., & Lorenzen, S. (2014). Writing in style. In R. Miller (Ed.), *Writing Fundamentals* (pp. 93-103). New York, NY: Anchor Press.

Chapter in Book with Seven Authors, Republished Date - Use the latest date listed

Whitters, M. J., Crossen, J. D., Matthews, P., Homes, R., Keller, J. R., Moreland, J. P., & Lorenzen, S. (2012). Writing in style. In R. Miller (Ed.), *APA made easy*. New York, NY: Anchor Press.

Chapter in Book with Seven Authors, Title with Subtitle

Whitters, M. J., Crossen, J. D., Matthews, P., Homes, R., Keller, J. R., Moreland, J. P., & Lorenzen, S. (2012). Writing in style. In R. Miller (Ed.), *APA made easy: A new way of formatting*. New York, NY: Anchor Press.

Chapter in Book, English Translation, Seven Authors

Whitters, M. J., Crossen, J. D., Matthews, P., Homes, R., Keller, J. R., Moreland, J. P., & Lorenzen, S. (2014). Creating a new metaphor (R. Miller, Trans.). In B. Reynolds (Ed.), *Formatting for dummies* (pp. 3-56). Dallas, TX: Anchor Press.

Chapter in Book with Seven Authors, Title with Proper Noun

Whitters, M. J., Crossen, J. D., Matthews, P., Homes, R., Keller, J. R., Moreland, J. P., & Lorenzen, S. (2014). Writing in style. In R. Miller (Ed.), *The life and times of J. Edgar Hoover.* New York, NY: Anchor Press.

Chapter in Book with Seven Authors, Limited Circulation, Not Online

Whitters, M. J., Crossen, J. D., Matthews, P., Homes, R., Keller, J. R., Moreland, J. P., & Lorenzen, S. (2014). Writing in style. In R. Miller (Ed.), *Creating a new metaphor.* (Available from Baker, 122 South Salem Street, Billings, MT. 59101)

Chapter in Book with Seven Authors, Limited Circulation, From Database - include URL of database where chapter can be found

Whitters, M. J., Crossen, J. D., Matthews, P., Homes, R., Keller, J. R., Moreland, J. P., & Lorenzen, S. (2014). Writing in style. In R. Miller (Ed.), *Creating a new metaphor.* Retrieved from http://www.nameofonlinedatabaseurl.edu/onlinelimitedcirculation

Chapter in Book, English Translation, Seven Authors

Whitters, M. J., Crossen, J. D., Matthews, P., Homes, R., Keller, J. R., Moreland, J. P., & Lorenzen, S. (2014). Creating a new metaphor (R. Miller, Trans.). In B. Reynolds (Ed.), *Formatting for dummies* (pp. 3-56). Dallas, TX: Anchor Press.

Chapter in Book, English Translation, Seven Authors, Reprinted from Another Source

Whitters, M. J., Crossen, J. D., Matthews, P., Homes, R., Keller, J. R., Moreland, J. P., & Lorenzen, S. (2014). Creating a new metaphor (R. Miller, Trans.). In B. Reynolds (Ed.), *Formatting for dummies* (pp. 3-56). Dallas, TX: Anchor Press. (Reprinted from *Formatting for fun*, pp. 78-121, by B. B. Newby, Ed., 2000, Billings, MT: Newport Press).

Book with Seven Authors, Ebook or Electronic Version

Whitters, M. J., Crossen, J. D., Matthews, P., Homes, R., Keller, J. R., Moreland, J. P., & Lorenzen, S. (2014). *Writing with style.* Retrieved from http://www.apamadeasy.com/ebooks

Book with Seven Authors, No Date, Ebook or Electronic Version

Whitters, M. J., Crossen, J. D., Matthews, P., Homes, R., Keller, J. R., Moreland, J. P., & Lorenzen, S. (n.d.). *Writing with style.* Retrieved from http://www.apamadeasy.com/ebooks

Book with Seven Authors, Ebook or Electronic Version, with DOI

Whitters, M. J., Crossen, J. D., Matthews, P., Homes, R., Keller, J. R., Moreland, J. P., & Lorenzen, S. (2014). *Writing with style.* doi:10.1234567890

Book with Seven Authors, Ebook or Electronic Version, Republished Date - Use the latest date listed

Whitters, M. J., Crossen, J. D., Matthews, P., Homes, R., Keller, J. R., Moreland, J. P., & Lorenzen, S. (2014). *Writing with style.* Retrieved from http://www.apamadeasy.com/ebooks

Book with Seven Authors, Ebook or Electronic Version, with DOI - Republished Date - Use the latest date listed

Whitters, M. J., Crossen, J. D., Matthews, P., Homes, R., Keller, J. R., Moreland, J. P., & Lorenzen, S. (2014). *Writing with style.* doi:10.1234567890

Book with Seven Authors, Ebook or Electronic Version, Edition Other Than First

Whitters, M. J., Crossen, J. D., Matthews, P., Homes, R., Keller, J. R., Moreland, J. P., & Lorenzen, S. (2012). *APA made easy* (4th ed.). Retrieved from http://www.apamadeasy.com/ebooks

Book with Seven Authors, Ebook or Electronic Version, Revised Edition

Whitters, M. J., Crossen, J. D., Matthews, P., Homes, R., Keller, J. R., Moreland, J. P., & Lorenzen, S. (2012). *APA made easy* (Rev. ed.). Retrieved from http://www.apamadeasy.com/ebooks

Book with Seven Authors, Ebook or Electronic Version, Title with Subtitle

Whitters, M. J., Crossen, J. D., Matthews, P., Homes, R., Keller, J. R., Moreland, J. P., & Lorenzen, S. (2012). *APA made easy: Writing with style.* Retrieved from http://www.apamadeasy.com/ebooks

Book with Seven Authors, Ebook or Electronic Version, No Date, Title with Subtitle

Whitters, M. J., Crossen, J. D., Matthews, P., Homes, R., Keller, J. R., Moreland, J. P., & Lorenzen, S. (n.d.). *APA made easy: Writing with style.* Retrieved from http://www.apamadeasy.com/ebooks

Book with Seven Authors, Ebook or Electronic Version, Title with Proper Noun

Whitters, M. J., Crossen, J. D., Matthews, P., Homes, R., Keller, J. R., Moreland, J. P., & Lorenzen, S. (2014). *The life and times of J. Edgar Hoover.* Retrieved from http://www.apamadeasy.com/ebooks

Book with Seven Authors, Ebook or Electronic Version, Title with Subtitle, Edition Other than First

Whitters, M. J., Crossen, J. D., Matthews, P., Homes, R., Keller, J. R., Moreland, J. P., & Lorenzen, S. (2014). *APA made easy: Writing with style* (4th ed.). Retrieved from http://www.apamadeasy.com/ebooks

Book with Seven Authors, Ebook or Electronic Version, No Date, Title with Subtitle, Edition Other than First

Whitters, M. J., Crossen, J. D., Matthews, P., Homes, R., Keller, J. R., Moreland, J. P., & Lorenzen, S. (n.d.). *APA made easy: Writing with style* (4th ed.). Retrieved from http://www.apamadeasy.com/ebooks

Book with Seven Authors, Ebook or Electronic Version, Title with Series

Whitters, M. J., Crossen, J. D., Matthews, P., Homes, R., Keller, J. R., Moreland, J. P., & Lorenzen, S. (2012). *APA made easy: Vol. 4. Writing with style.* Retrieved from http://www.apamadeasy.com/ebooks

Book with Seven Authors, Electronic Version of Print Version from E-Reader (Kindle, Nook, etc.) - Type of Electronic version goes in brackets

Whitters, M. J., Crossen, J. D., Matthews, P., Homes, R., Keller, J. R., Moreland, J. P., & Lorenzen, S. (2014). *APA made easy* [Kindle version]. Retrieved from http://www.youversustheworld.com/asp

Book with Seven Authors, Electronic Version of Republished Print Book

Whitters, M. J., Crossen, J. D., Matthews, P., Homes, R., Keller, J. R., Moreland, J. P., & Lorenzen, S. (2014). Writing in style. In R. Miller (Ed.), *Problem solving while writing long books* (pp. 80-88). Retrieved from http://www.youversustheworld.com/urlexamples (Original work published 2001)

Book with Seven Authors, Electronic Version of Republished Print Book, No Page Numbers Available

Whitters, M. J., Crossen, J. D., Matthews, P., Homes, R., Keller, J. R., Moreland, J. P., & Lorenzen, S. (2014). Writing in style. In R. Miller (Ed.), *Problem solving while writing long books*. Retrieved from http://www.youversustheworld.com/urlexamples

Chapter in Electronic Book/Ebook with Seven Authors

Whitters, M. J., Crossen, J. D., Matthews, P., Homes, R., Keller, J. R., Moreland, J. P., & Lorenzen, S. (2014). Writing in style. In R. Miller (Ed.), *Writing Fundamentals* (pp. 93-103). Retrieved from http://www.youversustheworld.com/chapterreferences

Chapter in Electronic Book/Ebook with Seven Authors, with DOI

Whitters, M. J., Crossen, J. D., Matthews, P., Homes, R., Keller, J. R., Moreland, J. P., & Lorenzen, S. (2014). Writing in style. In R. Miller (Ed.), *Writing Fundamentals* (pp. 93-103). doi:10.1234567890

Chapter in Electronic Book/Ebook with Seven Authors, Title with Subtitle

Whitters, M. J., Crossen, J. D., Matthews, P., Homes, R., Keller, J. R., Moreland, J. P., & Lorenzen, S. (2012). Writing in style. In R. Miller (Ed.), *APA made easy: A new way of formatting*. Retrieved from http://www.youversustheworld.com/chapterreferences

Chapter in Electronic Book/Ebook with Seven Authors, Republished Date - Use the latest date listed

Whitters, M. J., Crossen, J. D., Matthews, P., Homes, R., Keller, J. R., Moreland, J. P., & Lorenzen, S. (2012). Writing in style. In R. Miller (Ed.), *APA made easy*. Retrieved from http://www.youversustheworld.com/chapterreferences

Chapter in Electronic Book/Ebook with Seven Authors, Title with Subtitle, Republished Date - Use the latest date listed

Whitters, M. J., Crossen, J. D., Matthews, P., Homes, R., Keller, J. R., Moreland, J. P., & Lorenzen, S. (2012). Writing in style. In R. Miller (Ed.), *APA made easy: Writing with style*. Retrieved from http://www.youversustheworld.com/chapterreferences

Chapter in Electronic Book/Ebook of Print Version from Republished Book with Seven Authors, with Volume Number

Whitters, M. J., Crossen, J. D., Matthews, P., Homes, R., Keller, J. R., Moreland, J. P., & Lorenzen, S. (2014). Creating a new metaphor. In R. McClure (Ed.). *Writing with style* (Vol. 1, pp. 105-144). Retrieved from http://www.youversustheworld.com/ chapterreference

Chapter in Electronic Book/Ebook, English Translation, Seven Authors

Whitters, M. J., Crossen, J. D., Matthews, P., Homes, R., Keller, J. R., Moreland, J. P., & Lorenzen, S. (2014). Creating a new metaphor (R. Miller, Trans.). In B. Reynolds (Ed.), *Formatting for dummies* (pp. 3-56). Retrieved from http:// www.youversustheworld.com/chapterreferences

Chapter in Electronic Book/Ebook with Seven Authors, Title with Proper Noun

Whitters, M. J., Crossen, J. D., Matthews, P., Homes, R., Keller, J. R., Moreland, J. P., & Lorenzen, S. (2014). Writing in style. In R. Miller (Ed.), *The life and times of J. Edgar Hoover*. Retrieved from http://www.youversustheworld.com/chapterreferences

Chapter in Electronic Book/Ebook with Seven Authors, Limited Circulation, From Database - Include URL of database where chapter can be found

Whitters, M. J., Crossen, J. D., Matthews, P., Homes, R., Keller, J. R., Moreland, J. P., & Lorenzen, S. (2014). Writing in style. In R. Miller (Ed.), *Creating a new metaphor*. Retrieved from http://www.nameofonlinedatabaseurl.edu/onlinelimitedcirculation

Chapter in Electronic Book/Ebook, English Translation, Seven Authors

Whitters, M. J., Crossen, J. D., Matthews, P., Homes, R., Keller, J. R., Moreland, J. P., & Lorenzen, S. (2014). Creating a new metaphor (R. Miller, Trans.). In B. Reynolds (Ed.), *Formatting for dummies* (pp. 3-56). Retrieved from http://www.youversustheworld.com/chapterreferences

Chapter in Electronic Book/Ebook, English Translation, Seven Authors, Reprinted from Another Source

Whitters, M. J., Crossen, J. D., Matthews, P., Homes, R., Keller, J. R., Moreland, J. P., & Lorenzen, S. (2014). Creating a new metaphor (R. Miller, Trans.). In B. Reynolds (Ed.), *Formatting for dummies* (pp. 3-56). Retrieved from http://www.youversustheworld.com/chapterreferences (Reprinted from *Formatting for fun*, pp. 78-121, by B. B. Newby, Ed., 2000, Billings, MT: Newport Press).

Chapter in Electronic Book/Ebook of Print Version with Seven Authors (Kindle, Nook, etc.)

Whitters, M. J., Crossen, J. D., Matthews, P., Homes, R., Keller, J. R., Moreland, J. P., & Lorenzen, S. (2014). Creating a new metaphor. In R. McClure (Ed.). *Writing with style* [iBooks version]. Retrieved from http://www.ibooks.com/chapterreferences

Chapter in Electronic Book/Ebook of Print Version with Seven Authors, with DOI

Whitters, M. J., Crossen, J. D., Matthews, P., Homes, R., Keller, J. R., Moreland, J. P., & Lorenzen, S. (2014). Creating a new metaphor. In R. McClure (Ed.). *Writing with style* [iBooks version]. doi:10.1234567890

Reference Book with Seven Authors - Only list Editor's Name

Whitters, M. J., Crossen, J. D., Matthews, P., Homes, R., Keller, J. R., Moreland, J. P., & Lorenzen, S. (Ed.). (2014). *References in obscurity.* Wauconda, IL: Anchor Press.

Entry in Reference Book with Seven Authors

Whitters, M. J., Crossen, J. D., Matthews, P., Homes, R., Keller, J. R., Moreland, J. P., & Lorenzen, S. (2014). References in obscurity. In R. Miller (Ed.), *Getting references right* (3rd ed., Vol. 8). Wauconda, IL: Anchor Press.

Entry in Online Reference Book with Seven Authors

Whitters, M. J., Crossen, J. D., Matthews, P., Homes, R., Keller, J. R., Moreland, J. P., & Lorenzen, S. (2014). References in obscurity. In R. Miller (Ed.), *Getting references right* (3rd ed., Vol. 8). Retrieved from http://www.youversustheworld.com/referencesbooks

Entry in Online Reference Book with Seven Authors, with DOI

Whitters, M. J., Crossen, J. D., Matthews, P., Homes, R., Keller, J. R., Moreland, J. P., & Lorenzen, S. (2014). References in obscurity. In R. Miller (Ed.), *Getting references right* (3rd ed., Vol. 8). doi:10.1234567890

Entry in Online Reference Book with Seven Authors, with Page Numbers, with DOI

Whitters, M. J., Crossen, J. D., Matthews, P., Homes, R., Keller, J. R., Moreland, J. P., & Lorenzen, S. (2014). References in obscurity. In R. Miller (Ed.), *Getting references right* (pp. 251-298). doi:10.1234567890

Entry in Online Reference Book with Seven Authors, Alternative Edition Example

Whitters, M. J., Crossen, J. D., Matthews, P., Homes, R., Keller, J. R., Moreland, J. P., & Lorenzen, S. (2014). References in obscurity. In R. Miller (Ed.), *Getting references right* (Spring 2008 ed.). Retrieved from http://www.youversustheworld.com/referencesbooks

Books with Eight or More Authors

A Quick Overview : **Books with Eight or More Authors**

Sample Reference Structure:

Last Name, First Initial., Second Last Name, First Initial., Third Last Name, Third First Initial., Fifth Last Name, Fifth First Initial., Sixth Last Name, Sixth First Initial., . . . Eighth/Final Last Name, Eighth/Final First Initial. (Date of Publication). *Title of publication.* City, State Initials of Publication: Publisher.

Example:

Creston, J. P., Anders, R. F., Wilson, D. A., Peters, B. O., Roberts, M. A., Mathers, Y. O., . . . Nehman, T. (2012). *APA made easy.* New York, NY: Anchor Press.

Electronic Sample

Last Name, First Initial., Second Last Name, First Initial., Third Last Name, Third First Initial., Fifth Last Name, Fifth First Initial., Sixth Last Name, Sixth First Initial., . . . Eighth/Final Last Name, Eighth/Final First Initial. (Date of Publication). *Title of publication.* Retrieved from http://nameofurl.com

Electronic Example

Creston, J. P., Anders, R. F., Wilson, D. A., Peters, B. O., Roberts, M. A., Mathers, Y. O., . . . Nehman, T. (2014). *Writing with style.* Retrieved from http://www.apamadeasy.com/ebooks

Sample In-Text Citations

Example #1: Paraphrase

According to Anders et al. (2012), writing in APA format can be easy.

Example #2: Paraphrase

With so many resources available, writing in APA format can be easy (Anders et al., 2012).

Example #3: Direct Quote
Anders et al. (2012) stated, "Writing in APA format can be easy" (p. iv).

Example #4: Direct Quote
With so many resources available, writing in APA format can be easy (Anders et al., 2012, p. 16).

Books with Eight or More Authors

Book with Eight or More Authors, Standard Date of Publication

Creston, J. P., Anders, R. F., Wilson, D. A., Peters, B. O., Roberts, M. A., Mathers, Y. O., . . . Nehman, T. (2012). *APA made easy.* New York, NY: Anchor Press.

Book with Eight or More Authors, No Date

Creston, J. P., Anders, R. F., Wilson, D. A., Peters, B. O., Roberts, M. A., Mathers, Y. O., . . . Nehman, T. (n.d.). *APA made easy.* New York, NY: Anchor Press.

Book with Eight or More Authors, Republished Date - Use the latest date listed

Creston, J. P., Anders, R. F., Wilson, D. A., Peters, B. O., Roberts, M. A., Mathers, Y. O., . . . Nehman, T. (2012). *APA made easy.* New York, NY: Anchor Press.

In Text Citation Example - Cite both the original published date and the date of the republished version:
(Whitters et al., 2000/2012).

Book with Eight or More Authors, Edition Other Than First

Creston, J. P., Anders, R. F., Wilson, D. A., Peters, B. O., Roberts, M. A., Mathers, Y. O., . . . Nehman, T. (2012). *APA made easy* (4th ed.). New York, NY: Anchor Press.

Book with Eight or More Authors, Revised Edition

Creston, J. P., Anders, R. F., Wilson, D. A., Peters, B. O., Roberts, M. A., Mathers, Y. O., . . . Nehman, T. (2012). *APA made easy* (Rev. ed.). New York, NY: Anchor Press.

Book with Eight or More Authors, Title with Subtitle

Creston, J. P., Anders, R. F., Wilson, D. A., Peters, B. O., Roberts, M. A., Mathers, Y. O., . . . Nehman, T. (2012). *APA made easy: Writing with style.* New York, NY: Anchor Press.

Book with Eight or More Authors, No Date, Title with Subtitle

Creston, J. P., Anders, R. F., Wilson, D. A., Peters, B. O., Roberts, M. A., Mathers, Y. O., . . . Nehman, T. (n.d.). *APA made easy: Writing with style.* New York, NY: Anchor Press.

Book with Eight or More Authors, Title with Proper Noun

Creston, J. P., Anders, R. F., Wilson, D. A., Peters, B. O., Roberts, M. A., Mathers, Y. O., . . . Nehman, T. (2014). *The life and times of J. Edgar Hoover.* New York, NY: Anchor Press.

Book with Eight or More Authors, Title with Subtitle, Edition Other than First

Creston, J. P., Anders, R. F., Wilson, D. A., Peters, B. O., Roberts, M. A., Mathers, Y. O., . . . Nehman, T. (2014). *APA made easy: Writing with style* (4th ed.). New York, NY: Anchor Press.

Book with Eight or More Authors, No Date, Title with Subtitle, Edition Other than First

Creston, J. P., Anders, R. F., Wilson, D. A., Peters, B. O., Roberts, M. A., Mathers, Y. O., . . . Nehman, T. (n.d.). *APA made easy: Writing with style* (4th ed.). New York, NY: Anchor Press.

Book with Eight or More Authors, Title with Series

Creston, J. P., Anders, R. F., Wilson, D. A., Peters, B. O., Roberts, M. A., Mathers, Y. O., . . . Nehman, T. (2012). *APA made easy: Vol. 4. Writing with style.* New York, NY: Anchor Press.

Book with Eight or More Authors, Limited Circulation, Not Online

Creston, J. P., Anders, R. F., Wilson, D. A., Peters, B. O., Roberts, M. A., Mathers, Y. O., . . . Nehman, T. (2014). *Creating a new metaphor.* (Available from Baker, 122 South Salem Street, Billings, MT. 59101)

Book with Eight or More Authors, Limited Circulation, From Database

Creston, J. P., Anders, R. F., Wilson, D. A., Peters, B. O., Roberts, M. A., Mathers, Y. O., . . . Nehman, T. (2014). *Creating a new metaphor.* Retrieved from http://www.nameofonlinedatabaseurl.edu/onlinelimitedcirculation

Book with Eight or More Authors, Monograph

Creston, J. P., Anders, R. F., Wilson, D. A., Peters, B. O., Roberts, M. A., Mathers, Y. O., . . . Nehman, T. (2014). *Creating a new metaphor* [Monograph]. Retrieved from http://www.nameofonlinedatabaseurl.edu/onlinelimitedcirculation

Book with Eight or More Authors, No Date, Monograph

Creston, J. P., Anders, R. F., Wilson, D. A., Peters, B. O., Roberts, M. A., Mathers, Y. O., . . . Nehman, T. (n.d.). *Creating a new metaphor* [Monograph]. Retrieved from http://www.nameofonlinedatabaseurl.edu/onlinelimitedcirculation

Chapter in Book with Eight or More Authors

Creston, J. P., Anders, R. F., Wilson, D. A., Peters, B. O., Roberts, M. A., Mathers, Y. O., . . . Nehman, T. (2014). Writing in style. In R. Miller (Ed.), *Writing Fundamentals* (pp. 93-103). New York, NY: Anchor Press.

Chapter in Book with Eight or More Authors, Republished Date - Use the latest date listed

Creston, J. P., Anders, R. F., Wilson, D. A., Peters, B. O., Roberts, M. A., Mathers, Y. O., . . . Nehman, T. (2012). Writing in style. In R. Miller (Ed.), *APA made easy.* New York, NY: Anchor Press.

Chapter in Book with Eight or More Authors, Title with Subtitle

Creston, J. P., Anders, R. F., Wilson, D. A., Peters, B. O., Roberts, M. A., Mathers, Y. O., . . . Nehman, T. (2012). Writing in style. In R. Miller (Ed.), *APA made easy: A new way of formatting.* New York, NY: Anchor Press.

Chapter in Book, English Translation, Eight or More Authors

Creston, J. P., Anders, R. F., Wilson, D. A., Peters, B. O., Roberts, M. A., Mathers, Y. O., . . . Nehman, T. (2014). Creating a new metaphor (R. Miller, Trans.). In B. Reynolds (Ed.), *Formatting for dummies* (pp. 3-56). Dallas, TX: Anchor Press.

Chapter in Book with Eight or More Authors, Title with Proper Noun

Creston, J. P., Anders, R. F., Wilson, D. A., Peters, B. O., Roberts, M. A., Mathers, Y. O., . . . Nehman, T. (2014). Writing in style. In R. Miller (Ed.), *The life and times of J. Edgar Hoover.* New York, NY: Anchor Press.

Book with Seven Authors with Hyphenated Names

Anders, J.-R., Anders, R. F., Wilson, D. A., Peters, B. -O., Roberts, M. A., Mathers, Y. O., . . . Nehman, T. (2014). *The life and times of J. Edgar Hoover.* New York, NY: Anchor Press.

Chapter in Book with Eight or More Authors, Limited Circulation, Not Online

Creston, J. P., Anders, R. F., Wilson, D. A., Peters, B. O., Roberts, M. A., Mathers, Y. O., . . . Nehman, T. (2014). Writing in style. In R. Miller (Ed.), *Creating a new metaphor.* (Available from Baker, 122 South Salem Street, Billings, MT. 59101)

Chapter in Book with Eight or More Authors, Limited Circulation, From Database - include URL of database where chapter can be found

Creston, J. P., Anders, R. F., Wilson, D. A., Peters, B. O., Roberts, M. A., Mathers, Y. O., . . . Nehman, T. (2014). Writing in style. In R. Miller (Ed.), *Creating a new metaphor.* Retrieved from http://www.nameofonlinedatabaseurl.edu/onlinelimitedcirculation

Chapter in Book, English Translation, Eight or More Authors

Creston, J. P., Anders, R. F., Wilson, D. A., Peters, B. O., Roberts, M. A., Mathers, Y. O., . . . Nehman, T. (2014). Creating a new metaphor (R. Miller, Trans.). In B. Reynolds (Ed.), *Formatting for dummies* (pp. 3-56). Dallas, TX: Anchor Press.

Chapter in Book, English Translation, Eight or More Authors, Reprinted from Another Source

Creston, J. P., Anders, R. F., Wilson, D. A., Peters, B. O., Roberts, M. A., Mathers, Y. O., . . . Nehman, T. (2014). Creating a new metaphor (R. Miller, Trans.). In B. Reynolds (Ed.), *Formatting for dummies* (pp. 3-56). Dallas, TX: Anchor Press. (Reprinted from *Formatting for fun*, pp. 78-121, by B. B. Newby, Ed., 2000, Billings, MT: Newport Press).

Book with Eight or More Authors, Ebook or Electronic Version

Creston, J. P., Anders, R. F., Wilson, D. A., Peters, B. O., Roberts, M. A., Mathers, Y. O., . . . Nehman, T. (2014). *Writing with style.* Retrieved from http://www.apamadeasy.com/ebooks

Book with Eight or More Authors, No Date, Ebook or Electronic Version

Creston, J. P., Anders, R. F., Wilson, D. A., Peters, B. O., Roberts, M. A., Mathers, Y. O., . . . Nehman, T. (n.d.). *Writing with style.* Retrieved from http://www.apamadeasy.com/ebooks

Book with Eight or More Authors, Ebook or Electronic Version, with DOI

Creston, J. P., Anders, R. F., Wilson, D. A., Peters, B. O., Roberts, M. A., Mathers, Y. O., . . . Nehman, T. (2014). *Writing with style.* doi:10.1234567890

Book with Eight or More Authors, Ebook or Electronic Version, Republished Date - Use the latest date listed

Creston, J. P., Anders, R. F., Wilson, D. A., Peters, B. O., Roberts, M. A., Mathers, Y. O., . . . Nehman, T. (2014). *Writing with style.* Retrieved from http://www.apamadeasy.com/ebooks

Book with Eight or More Authors, Ebook or Electronic Version, with DOI - Republished Date - Use the latest date listed

Creston, J. P., Anders, R. F., Wilson, D. A., Peters, B. O., Roberts, M. A., Mathers, Y. O., . . . Nehman, T. (2014). *Writing with style.* doi:10.1234567890

Book with Eight or More Authors, Ebook or Electronic Version, Edition Other Than First

Creston, J. P., Anders, R. F., Wilson, D. A., Peters, B. O., Roberts, M. A., Mathers, Y. O., . . . Nehman, T. (2012). *APA made easy* (4th ed.). Retrieved from http://www.apamadeasy.com/ebooks

Book with Eight or More Authors, Ebook or Electronic Version, Revised Edition

Creston, J. P., Anders, R. F., Wilson, D. A., Peters, B. O., Roberts, M. A., Mathers, Y. O., . . . Nehman, T. (2012). *APA made easy* (Rev. ed.). Retrieved from http://www.apamadeasy.com/ebooks

Book with Eight or More Authors, Ebook or Electronic Version, Title with Subtitle

Creston, J. P., Anders, R. F., Wilson, D. A., Peters, B. O., Roberts, M. A., Mathers, Y. O., . . . Nehman, T. (2012). *APA made easy: Writing with style.* Retrieved from http://www.apamadeasy.com/ebooks

Book with Eight or More Authors, Ebook or Electronic Version, No Date, Title with Subtitle

Creston, J. P., Anders, R. F., Wilson, D. A., Peters, B. O., Roberts, M. A., Mathers, Y. O., . . . Nehman, T. (n.d.). *APA made easy: Writing with style.* Retrieved from http://www.apamadeasy.com/ebooks

Book with Eight or More Authors, Ebook or Electronic Version, Title with Proper Noun

Creston, J. P., Anders, R. F., Wilson, D. A., Peters, B. O., Roberts, M. A., Mathers, Y. O., . . . Nehman, T. (2014). *The life and times of J. Edgar Hoover.* Retrieved from http://www.apamadeasy.com/ebooks

Book with Eight or More Authors, Ebook or Electronic Version, Title with Subtitle, Edition Other than First

Creston, J. P., Anders, R. F., Wilson, D. A., Peters, B. O., Roberts, M. A., Mathers, Y. O., . . . Nehman, T. (2014). *APA made easy: Writing with style* (4th ed.). Retrieved from http://www.apamadeasy.com/ebooks

Book with Eight or More Authors, Ebook or Electronic Version, No Date, Title with Subtitle, Edition Other than First

Creston, J. P., Anders, R. F., Wilson, D. A., Peters, B. O., Roberts, M. A., Mathers, Y. O., . . . Nehman, T. (n.d.). *APA made easy: Writing with style* (4th ed.). Retrieved from http://www.apamadeasy.com/ebooks

Book with Eight or More Authors, Ebook or Electronic Version, Title with Series

Creston, J. P., Anders, R. F., Wilson, D. A., Peters, B. O., Roberts, M. A., Mathers, Y. O., . . . Nehman, T. (2012). *APA made easy: Vol. 4. Writing with style.* Retrieved from http://www.apamadeasy.com/ebooks

Book with Eight or More Authors, Electronic Version of Print Version from E-Reader (Kindle, Nook, etc.) - Type of Electronic version goes in brackets

Creston, J. P., Anders, R. F., Wilson, D. A., Peters, B. O., Roberts, M. A., Mathers, Y. O., . . . Nehman, T. (2014). *APA made easy* [Kindle version]. Retrieved from http://www.youversustheworld.com/asp

Book with Eight or More Authors, Electronic Version of Republished Print Book

Creston, J. P., Anders, R. F., Wilson, D. A., Peters, B. O., Roberts, M. A., Mathers, Y. O., . . . Nehman, T. (2014). Writing in style. In R. Miller (Ed.), *Problem solving while writing long books* (pp. 80-88). Retrieved from http://www.youversustheworld.com/urlexamples (Original work published 2001)

Book with Eight or More Authors, Electronic Version of Republished Print Book, No Page Numbers Available

Creston, J. P., Anders, R. F., Wilson, D. A., Peters, B. O., Roberts, M. A., Mathers, Y. O., . . . Nehman, T. (2014). Writing in style. In R. Miller (Ed.), *Problem solving while writing long books*. Retrieved from http://www.youversustheworld.com/urlexamples

Chapter in Electronic Book/Ebook with Eight or More Authors

Creston, J. P., Anders, R. F., Wilson, D. A., Peters, B. O., Roberts, M. A., Mathers, Y. O., . . . Nehman, T. (2014). Writing in style. In R. Miller (Ed.), *Writing Fundamentals* (pp. 93-103). Retrieved from http://www.youversustheworld.com/chapterreferences

Chapter in Electronic Book/Ebook with Eight or More Authors, with DOI

Creston, J. P., Anders, R. F., Wilson, D. A., Peters, B. O., Roberts, M. A., Mathers, Y. O., . . . Nehman, T. (2014). Writing in style. In R. Miller (Ed.), *Writing Fundamentals* (pp. 93-103). doi:10.1234567890

Chapter in Electronic Book/Ebook with Eight or More Authors, Title with Subtitle

Creston, J. P., Anders, R. F., Wilson, D. A., Peters, B. O., Roberts, M. A., Mathers, Y. O., . . . Nehman, T. (2012). Writing in style. In R. Miller (Ed.), *APA made easy: A new way of formatting*. Retrieved from http://www.youversustheworld.com/chapterreferences

Chapter in Electronic Book/Ebook with Eight or More Authors, Republished Date - Use the latest date listed

Creston, J. P., Anders, R. F., Wilson, D. A., Peters, B. O., Roberts, M. A., Mathers, Y. O., . . . Nehman, T. (2012). Writing in style. In R. Miller (Ed.), *APA made easy*. Retrieved from http://www.youversustheworld.com/chapterreferences

Chapter in Electronic Book/Ebook with Eight or More Authors, Title with Subtitle, Republished Date - Use the latest date listed

Creston, J. P., Anders, R. F., Wilson, D. A., Peters, B. O., Roberts, M. A., Mathers, Y. O., . . . Nehman, T. (2012). Writing in style. In R. Miller (Ed.), *APA made easy: Writing with style*. Retrieved from http://www.youversustheworld.com/chapterreferences

Chapter in Electronic Book/Ebook of Print Version from Republished Book with Eight or More Authors, with Volume Number

Creston, J. P., Anders, R. F., Wilson, D. A., Peters, B. O., Roberts, M. A., Mathers, Y. O., . . . Nehman, T. (2014). Creating a new metaphor. In R. McClure (Ed.). *Writing with style* (Vol. 1, pp. 105-144). Retrieved from http://www.youversustheworld.com/chapterreference

Chapter in Electronic Book/Ebook, English Translation, Eight or More Authors

Creston, J. P., Anders, R. F., Wilson, D. A., Peters, B. O., Roberts, M. A., Mathers, Y. O., . . . Nehman, T. (2014). Creating a new metaphor (R. Miller, Trans.). In B. Reynolds (Ed.), *Formatting for dummies* (pp. 3-56). Retrieved from http://www.youversustheworld.com/chapterreferences

Chapter in Electronic Book/Ebook with Eight or More Authors, Title with Proper Noun

Creston, J. P., Anders, R. F., Wilson, D. A., Peters, B. O., Roberts, M. A., Mathers, Y. O., . . . Nehman, T. (2014). Writing in style. In R. Miller (Ed.), *The life and times of J. Edgar Hoover*. Retrieved from http://www.youversustheworld.com/chapterreferences

Chapter in Electronic Book/Ebook with Eight or More Authors, Limited Circulation, From Database - Include URL of database where chapter can be found

Creston, J. P., Anders, R. F., Wilson, D. A., Peters, B. O., Roberts, M. A., Mathers, Y. O., . . . Nehman, T. (2014). Writing in style. In R. Miller (Ed.), *Creating a new metaphor.* Retrieved from http://www.nameofonlinedatabaseurl.edu/onlinelimitedcirculation

Chapter in Electronic Book/Ebook, English Translation, Eight or More Authors

Creston, J. P., Anders, R. F., Wilson, D. A., Peters, B. O., Roberts, M. A., Mathers, Y. O., . . . Nehman, T. (2014). Creating a new metaphor (R. Miller, Trans.). In B. Reynolds (Ed.), *Formatting for dummies* (pp. 3-56). Retrieved from http://www.youversustheworld.com/chapterreferences

Chapter in Electronic Book/Ebook, English Translation, Eight or More Authors, Reprinted from Another Source

Creston, J. P., Anders, R. F., Wilson, D. A., Peters, B. O., Roberts, M. A., Mathers, Y. O., . . . Nehman, T. (2014). Creating a new metaphor (R. Miller, Trans.). In B. Reynolds (Ed.), *Formatting for dummies* (pp. 3-56). Retrieved from http://www.youversustheworld.com/chapterreferences (Reprinted from *Formatting for fun*, pp. 78-121, by B. B. Newby, Ed., 2000, Billings, MT: Newport Press).

Chapter in Electronic Book/Ebook of Print Version with Eight or More Authors (Kindle, Nook, etc.)

Creston, J. P., Anders, R. F., Wilson, D. A., Peters, B. O., Roberts, M. A., Mathers, Y. O., . . . Nehman, T. (2014). Creating a new metaphor. In R. McClure (Ed.). *Writing with style* [iBooks version]. Retrieved from http://www.ibooks.com/chapterreferences

Chapter in Electronic Book/Ebook of Print Version with Eight or More Authors, with DOI

Creston, J. P., Anders, R. F., Wilson, D. A., Peters, B. O., Roberts, M. A., Mathers, Y. O., . . . Nehman, T. (2014). Creating a new metaphor. In R. McClure (Ed.). *Writing with style* [iBooks version]. doi:10.1234567890

Reference Book with Eight or More Authors - Only list Editor's Name

Creston, J. P., Anders, R. F., Wilson, D. A., Peters, B. O., Roberts, M. A., Mathers, Y. O., . . . Nehman, T. (Ed.). (2014). *References in obscurity*. Wauconda, IL: Anchor Press.

Entry in Reference Book with Eight or More Authors

Creston, J. P., Anders, R. F., Wilson, D. A., Peters, B. O., Roberts, M. A., Mathers, Y. O., . . . Nehman, T. (2014). References in obscurity. In R. Miller (Ed.), *Getting references right* (3rd ed., Vol. 8). Wauconda, IL: Anchor Press.

Entry in Online Reference Book with Eight or More Authors

Creston, J. P., Anders, R. F., Wilson, D. A., Peters, B. O., Roberts, M. A., Mathers, Y. O., . . . Nehman, T. (2014). References in obscurity. In R. Miller (Ed.), *Getting references right* (3rd ed., Vol. 8). Retrieved from http://www.youversustheworld.com/ referencesbooks

Entry in Online Reference Book with Eight or More Authors, with DOI

Creston, J. P., Anders, R. F., Wilson, D. A., Peters, B. O., Roberts, M. A., Mathers, Y. O., . . . Nehman, T. (2014). References in obscurity. In R. Miller (Ed.), *Getting references right* (3rd ed., Vol. 8). doi:10.1234567890

Entry in Online Reference Book with Eight or More Authors, with Page Numbers, with DOI

Creston, J. P., Anders, R. F., Wilson, D. A., Peters, B. O., Roberts, M. A., Mathers, Y. O., . . . Nehman, T. (2014). References in obscurity. In R. Miller (Ed.), *Getting references right* (pp. 251-298). doi:10.1234567890

Entry in Online Reference Book with Eight or More Authors, Alternative Edition Example

Creston, J. P., Anders, R. F., Wilson, D. A., Peters, B. O., Roberts, M. A., Mathers, Y. O., . . . Nehman, T. (2014). References in obscurity. In R. Miller (Ed.), *Getting references right* (Spring 2008 ed.). Retrieved from http://www.youversustheworld.com/ referencesbooks

Chapter 2 - References for Periodicals - Journals, Magazines, Newspapers, and Newsletters

Periodicals Without An Author

A Quick Overview : **Periodicals without an Author**

Sample Reference Structure

Title of article (Year of Publication). *Title of Periodical, Periodical number,* Page numbers.

Example:

Formatting for beginners. (2014). *Journal of Writing, 44,* 77-88.

Electronic Sample

Title of article (Year of Publication). *Title of Periodical, Periodical number,* Page numbers. doi: xx-xxxxxxxxxx

Electronic Example

Formatting for beginners. (2014). *Journal of Writing, 44,* 77-88. doi: 10.1234567890

Sample In-Text Citations

For periodicals with no author, we put the name or shortened name (if the title is long) in quotations followed by a comma and the year of publication. ("Formatting for", 2014).

Alternatively, you may include the title of the article in the text of your paper, then follow it with the date in parenthesis:

Formatting for Beginners (2014) claims that …

Periodicals without an Author

Print Periodical, No Author, Arranged by Volume Number

Formatting for beginners. (2014). *Journal of Writing, 44,* 77-88.

Print periodical, No Author, No Date, Arranged by Volume Number

Formatting for beginners. (n.d.). *Journal of Writing, 44,* 77-88.

Print Periodical, No Author, Arranged by Issue Number

Formatting for beginners. (2014). *Journal of Writing, 44*(3), 77-88.

Print Periodical, No Author, No Date, Arranged by Issue Number

Formatting for beginners. (n.d.). *Journal of Writing, 44*(3), 77-88.

Print Periodical, No Author, with Editor

Anders, J. (Ed.). (2014). Writing in a British accent. *Journal Title is Capitalized, 14*(8).

Print Periodical, No Author, with Two Editors

Anders, J., & Beiler, R. (Eds.). (2014). Writing in a British accent. *Journal Title is Capitalized, 14*(8).

Title Translated Into English, No Author

Seja Feliz [Be happy]. (2014). *Bondade E' A Resposta, 6,* 12-18.

Newspaper Article, No Author

Formatting for beginners. (2014). *The Denver Post,* pp. A3, A4.

Editorial, No Author

Editorial: Formatting for fun [Editorial]. (2014). *Journal of Editing, 6,* 13-15.

Online Journal Article, No Author (Article Title Goes First), with DOI

Formatting for beginners. (2014). *Journal of Writing, 44,* 77-88. doi: 10.1234567890

Online Journal Article, No Author, No Date (Article Title Goes First), with DOI

Formatting for beginners. (n.d.). *Journal of Writing, 44,* 77-88. doi: 10.1234567890

Online Journal Article, No Author, Arranged by Issue Number (Follows Volume Number), with DOI

Formatting for beginners. (2014). *Journal of Writing, 44*(3), 77-88. doi: 10.1234567890

Online Journal Article with No Author, No Date, Arranged by Issue Number (Follows Volume Number) with DOI

Formatting for beginners. (n.d.). *Journal of Writing, 44*(3), 77-88. doi: 10.1234567890

Online Journal Article, No Author, No DOI

Formatting for beginners. (2014). *Journal of Writing, 44*, 77-88. Retrieved from http://www.youversustheworld.com

Online Journal Article, No Author, No Date, No DOI

Formatting for beginners. (n.d.). *Journal of Writing, 44*, 77-88. Retrieved from http://www.youversustheworld.com

Online Journal Article, No Author, One Editor, No DOI

Anders, J. (Ed.). (2014). Writing in a British accent. *Journal Title is Capitalized, 14*(8). Retrieved from http:www.youversustheworld.com

Online Journal Article, No Author, with Two Editors, No DOI

Anders, J., & Beiler, R. (Eds.). (2014). Writing in a British accent. *Journal Title is Capitalized, 14*(8). Retrieved from http://www.youversustheworld.com

Online Journal Article, No Author, One Editor, with DOI

Anders, J. (Ed.). (2014). Writing in a British accent. *Journal Title is Capitalized, 14*(8). doi: 10.1234567890

Online Journal Article, No Author, with Two Editors, with DOI

Anders, J., & Beiler, R. (Eds.). (2014). Writing in a British accent. *Journal Title is Capitalized, 14*(8). doi:10.1234567890

Online Journal Article, No Author, Arranged by Issue Number (Follows Volume Number), with DOI

Formatting for beginners. (2014). *Journal of Writing, 44*(3), 77-88. doi: 10.1234567890

Online Journal Article, No Author, No Date, Arranged by Issue Number (Follows Volume Number), with DOI

Formatting for beginners. (n.d.). *Journal of Writing, 44*(3), 77-88. doi:10.1234567890

Online Journal Article, No Author, Arranged by Issue Number (Follows Volume Number), No DOI

Formatting for beginners. (2014). *Journal of Writing, 44*(3), 77-88. Retrieved from http://www.youversustheworld.com

Online Journal Article, No Author, No Date, Arranged by Issue Number (Follows Volume Number) No DOI

Formatting for beginners. (n.d.). *Journal of Writing, 44*(3), 77-88. Retrieved from http://www.youversustheworld.com

Online Journal Article, No Author, Found in Library Database

Formatting for beginners. (2014). *Journal of Writing, 44,* 77-88. Retrieved from EBSCO MegaFile Database.

Journal Article, No Author, No Date, Found in Library Database

Formatting for beginners. (n.d.). *Journal of Writing, 44,* 77-88. Retrieved from www.urlofdatabase.edu

***Note that the APA Manual does not suggest including database information in your reference as database information changes frequently. If you need to include database information, use the url where you found the article that you are citing. In this case, using a DOI is always preferable.

Journal Article, No Author, Advance Online Publication, no DOI

Formatting for beginners. (2014). *Journal of Writing,* Advance online publication. Retrieved from http://www.youversustheworld.com

Journal Article, No Author, No Date, Advance Online Publication, no DOI

Formatting for beginners. (n.d.). *Journal of Writing,* Advance online publication. Retrieved from http://www.youversustheworld.com

Journal Article, No Author, In Press

Formatting for beginners. (in press). *Journal of Writing.* Retrieved from http://www.youversustheworld.com

Journal Abstract as Original Source, No Author, no DOI

Formatting for beginners. (2014). Formatting for beginners. *Journal of Writing, 44,* 77-88. Abstract retrieved from http://www.youversustheworld.com

Journal Abstract as Secondary Source, No Author, no DOI

Formatting for beginners. (2014). *Journal of Writing, 44,* 77-88. Abstract retrieved from Name of Large Database. (Accenssion No. 123456789)

Journal Article, No Author, Translated Into English

Seja felix [Be happy]. (2014). *Bondade E' A Resposta, 6,* 12-18. Retrieved from http://www.youversustheworld.com

Online Newspaper Article, No Author.

Formatting for beginners. (2014). *The Denver Post,* pp. A3, A4. Retrieved from www.denverpost.com

Editorial Online, No Author

Editorial: Formatting for fun [Editorial]. (2014). *Journal of Editing.* Retrieved from http:www.youversustheworld.com

Newsletter, No Author

Winning is fun. (2014, May/June). *Corporate Italicized News.* Retrieved from http://www.exacturlifpossible.com/html/news/may/newsletter

In Text Citation Example:

("Winning," 2014).

Newsletter, No Author, Exact Publication Date

Winning is fun. (2014, May 6). *Corporate Italicized News.* Retrieved from http://www.exacturlifpossible.com/html/news/may/newsletter

152

Newsletter, No Author, with DOI

Winning is fun. (2014, May/June). *Corporate Italicized News.* doi:10.1234567890

Periodicals With One Author

A Quick Overview : ***Periodicals with One Author***

Sample Reference Structure

Author Last Name, First Initial. (Year of Publication). Name of article. *Title of Periodical, Periodical number,* Page numbers.

Example:

Anders, J. C. (2014). Formatting for beginners. *Journal of Writing, 44*, 77-88.

Electronic Sample

Author Last Name, First Initial. (Year of Publication). Name of article. *Title of Periodical, Periodical number,* Page numbers. doi: xx-xxxxxxxxxx

Electronic Example

Anders, J. C. (2014). Formatting for beginners. *Journal of Writing, 44*, 77-88. doi: 10.1234567890

Sample In-Text Citations

Example #1: Paraphrase

According to Anders (2012), writing in APA format can be easy.

Example #2: Paraphrase

With so many resources available, writing in APA format can be easy (Anders, 2012).

Example #3: Direct Quote

Anders (2012) stated, "Writing in APA format can be easy" (p. iv).

Example #4: Direct Quote

With so many resources available, writing in APA format can be easy (Anders, 2012, p. 19).

Periodicals with One Author

Print Periodical, One Author, Arranged by Volume Number

Anders, J. C. (2014). Formatting for beginners. *Journal of Writing, 44*, 77-88.

Print Periodical, One Author, No Date, Arranged by Volume Number

Anders, J. C. (n.d.). Formatting for beginners. *Journal of Writing, 44*, 77-88.

Print Periodical, One Author, Arranged by Issue Number

Anders, J. C. (2014). Formatting for beginners. *Journal of Writing, 44*(3), 77-88.

Print Periodical, One Author, No Date, Arranged by Issue Number

Anders, J. C. (n.d.). Formatting for beginners. *Journal of Writing, 44*(3), 77-88.

Print Periodical, One Author, In Press

Anders, J. C. (in press). Formatting for beginners. *Journal of Writing, 44*(3), 77-88.

Print Periodical, One Author, Translated Into English

Guerrimo, R. (2014). Seja felix [Be happy]. *Bondade E' A Resposta, 6*, 12-18.

Supplemental Material in Journal, Online

Anders, J. C. (2014). Formatting for beginners [Supplemental material]. *Journal of Writing, 79,* 125-141. http://dx.doi.or/10.1234567890

Print Periodical, One Author, with Special Issue

Anders, J. C. (2014). Writing articles in euphoric state [Special issue]. *Righting Writers' Wrongs, 14*(8).

Print Periodical, One Author, with Special Section

Anders, J. C. (2014). Writing articles in euphoric state [Special section]. *Righting Writers' Wrongs, 14*(8).

Newspaper Article, One Author

Anders, J. (2014). Formatting for beginners. *The Denver Post,* pp. A3, A4.

Editorial, One Author

Anders, J. (2014). Formatting for fun [Editorial]. *Journal of Editing, 6,* 13-15

Online Journal Article, One Author, With DOI

Anders, J. C. (2014). Formatting for beginners. *Journal of Writing, 44,* 77-88. doi: 10.1234567890

Online Journal Article, One Author, No Date, With DOI

Anders, J. C. (n.d.). Formatting for beginners. *Journal of Writing, 44,* 77-88. doi: 10.1234567890

Online Journal Article, One Author, Arranged by Issue Number, with DOI

Anders, J. C. (2014). *Journal of Writing, 44*(3), 77-88. doi: 10.1234567890

Online Journal Article, One Author, No Date, Arranged by Issue Number, with DOI

Anders, J. C. (n.d.). *Journal of Writing, 44*(3), 77-88. doi: 10.1234567890

Online Journal Article, One Author, Found in Library Database, with DOI

Anders, J. C. (2014). Formatting for beginners. *Journal of Writing, 44,* 77-88. doi: 10.1234567890

Online Journal Article, One Author, No Date, Found in Library Database, with DOI

Anders, J. C. (n.d.). Formatting for beginners. *Journal of Writing, 44,* 77-88. doi: 10.1234567890

Online Journal Article, One Author, Advance Online Publication, with DOI

Anders, J. C., & Beiler, R. C. (2014). Formatting for beginners. *Journal of Writing,* Advance online publication. doi: 10.1234567890

Online Journal Article, One Author, No Date, Advance Online Publication, with DOI

Anders, J. C., & Beiler, R. C. (n.d.). Formatting for beginners. *Journal of Writing,* Advance online publication. doi: 10.1234567890

Online Journal Article, One Author, no DOI

Anders, J. C. (2014). Formatting for beginners. *Journal of Writing, 44,* 77-88. Retrieved from http://www.youversustheworld.com

Online Journal Article, One Author, no Date, no DOI

Anders, J. C. (n.d.). Formatting for beginners. *Journal of Writing, 44,* 77-88. Retrieved from http://www.youversustheworld.com/

Online Journal Article, One Author, Arranged by Issue Number, no DOI

Anders, J. C. (2014). *Journal of Writing, 44*(3), 77-88. Retrieved from http://www.youversustheworld.com

Online Journal Article, One Author, No Date, Arranged by Issue Number, no DOI

Anders, J. C. (n.d.). *Journal of Writing, 44*(3), 77-88. Retrieved from http://www.youversustheworld.com/

Online Journal Article, One Author, Found in Library Database

Anders, J. C. (2014). Formatting for beginners. *Journal of Writing, 44,* 77-88. Retrieved from http://www.urlofdatabase.com

Online Journal Article, One Author, No Date, Found in Library Database

Anders, J. C. (n.d.). Formatting for beginners. *Journal of Writing, 44,* 77-88. Retrieved from http://www.urlofdatabase.com

***Note that the APA Manual does not suggest including database information in your reference as database information changes frequently. If you need to include database information, use the url where you found the article that you are citing. In this case, using a DOI is always preferable.

Online Journal Article, One Author, Advance Online Publication, no DOI

Anders, J. C. (2014). Formatting for beginners. *Journal of Writing,* Advance online publication. Retrieved from http://www.youversustheworld.com

Online Journal Article, One Author, No Date, Advance Online Publication, no DOI

Anders, J. C. (n.d.). Formatting for beginners. *Journal of Writing,* Advance online publication. Retrieved from http://www.youversustheworld.com

Online Journal Article, One Author, In Press

Anders, J. C. (in press). Formatting for beginners. *Journal of Writing.* Retrieved from http://www.youversustheworld.com

Journal Abstract as Original Source, One Author, no DOI

Anders, J. C. (2014). Formatting for beginners. *Journal of Writing, 44,* 77-88. Abstract retrieved from http://www.youversustheworld.com

Journal Abstract as Secondary Source, One Author, no DOI

Anders, J. C. (2014). Formatting for beginners. *Journal of Writing, 44,* 77-88. Abstract retrieved from Name of Large Database. (Accenssion No. 123456789)

Online Journal Article, One Author, Translated Into English

Guerrimo, R. (2014). Seja felix [Be happy]. *Bondade E' A Resposta, 6,* 12-18. Retrieved from http://www.youversustheworld.com

Supplemental Material in Journal, Online

Anders, J. C. (2014). Formatting for beginners [Supplemental material]. *Journal of Writing, 79,* 125-141. http://dx.doi.or/10.1234567890

Online Journal Article, One Author, with Special Issue

Anders, J. C. (2014). Writing articles in euphoric state [Special issue]. *Righting Writers' Wrongs, 14*(8).

Online Newspaper Article, One Author

Anders, J. (2014). Formatting for beginners. *The Denver Post,* pp. A3, A4. Retrieved from www.denverpost.com

Editorial Online, One Author

Anders, J. (2014). Formatting for fun [Editorial]. *Journal of Editing, 6,* 13-15. Retrieved from http://www.youversutheworld.com

Editorial Online, One Author, with DOI

Anders, J. (2014). Formatting for fun [Editorial]. *Journal of Editing, 6,* 13-15. doi: 10.1234567890

Newsletter, One Author

Anders, J. (2014, May/June). Winning is fun. *Corporate Italicized News.* Retrieved from http://www.exacturlifpossible.com/html/news/may/newsletter

Newsletter, One Author, Exact Publication Date

Anders, J. (2014, May 6). Winning is fun. *Corporate Italicized News.* Retrieved from http://www.exacturlifpossible.com/html/news/may/newsletter

Newsletter, One Author, with DOI

Anders, J. (2014, May/June). Winning is fun. *Corporate Italicized News.* doi: 10.1234567890

Periodicals With Two Authors

A Quick Overview : **Periodicals with Two Authors**

Sample Reference Structure

Author Last Name, First Initial., & Second Last Name, First Initial. (Year of Publication). Name of article. *Title of Periodical, Periodical number,* Page numbers.

Example:

Anders, J. C., & Beiler, R. C. (2014). Formatting for beginners. *Journal of Writing, 44,* 77-88.

Electronic Sample

Author Last Name, First Initial., & Second Last Name, First Initial. (Year of Publication). Name of article. *Title of Periodical, Periodical number,* Page numbers. doi: xx-xxxxxxxxxx

Electronic Example

Anders, J. C., & Beiler, R. C. (2014). Formatting for beginners. *Journal of Writing, 44,* 77-88. doi: 10.1234567890

Sample In-Text Citations

Example #1: Paraphrase

According to Anders & Beiler (2012), writing in APA format can be easy.

Example #2: Paraphrase

With so many resources available, writing in APA format can be easy (Anders & Beiler, 2012).

Example #3: Direct Quote

Anders & Beiler (2012) stated, "Writing in APA format can be easy" (p. iv).

Example #4: Direct Quote

With so many resources available, writing in APA format can be easy (Anders & Beiler, 2012, p. 19).

Print Periodical with Two Authors

Print Periodical, Two Authors, Arranged by Volume Number

Anders, J. C., & Beiler, R. C. (2014). Formatting for beginners. *Journal of Writing, 44,* 77-88.

Print Periodical, Two Authors, No Date, Arranged by Volume Number

Anders, J. C., & Beiler, R. C. (n.d.). Formatting for beginners. *Journal of Writing, 44,* 77-88.

Print Periodical, Two Authors, Arranged by Issue Number

Anders, J. C., & Beiler, R. C. (2014). Formatting for beginners. *Journal of Writing, 44*(3), 77-88.

Print Periodical, Two Authors, No Date, Arranged by Issue Number

Anders, J. C., & Beiler, R. C. (n.d.). Formatting for beginners. *Journal of Writing, 44*(3), 77-88.

Print Periodical, Two Authors, In Press

Anders, J. C., & Beiler, R. C. (in press). Formatting for beginners. *Journal of Writing, 44,* 77-88.

Print Periodical, Two Authors, Translated Into English

Anders, J. C., & Beiler, R. C. (2014). Seja felix [Be happy]. *Bondade E' A Resposta, 6,* 12-18.

Supplemental Material in Journal, Online

Anders, J. C., & Beiler, R. C. (2014). Formatting for beginners [Supplemental material]. *Journal of Writing, 79,* 125-141. http://dx.doi.or/10.1234567890

Print Periodical, Two Authors, with Special Issue

Anders, J. C., & Beiler, R. C. (2014). Writing articles in euphoric state [Special issue]. *Righting Writers' Wrongs, 14*(8).

Print Periodical, Two Authors, with Special Section

Anders, J. C., & Beiler, R. C. (2014). Writing articles in euphoric state [Special section]. *Righting Writers' Wrongs, 14*(8).

Newspaper Article, Two Authors

Anders, J., & Beiler, R. (2014). Formatting for beginners. *The Denver Post,* pp. A3, A4.

Editorial, Two Authors

Anders, J. C., & Beiler, R. C. (2014). Formatting for fun [Editorial]. *Journal of Editing, 6,* 13-15.

Journal Article, Two Authors, With DOI

Anders, J. C., & Beiler, R. C. (2014). Formatting for beginners. *Journal of Writing, 44,* 77-88. doi: 10.1234567890

Journal Article, Two Authors, No Date, With DOI

Anders, J. C., & Beiler, R. C. (n.d.). Formatting for beginners. *Journal of Writing, 44,* 77-88. doi: 10.1234567890

Journal Article, Two Authors, Arranged by Issue Number, with DOI

Anders, J. C., & Beiler, R. C. (2014). *Journal of Writing, 44*(3), 77-88. doi: 10.1234567890

Journal Article, Two Authors, No Date, Arranged by Issue Number, with DOI

Anders, J. C., & Beiler, R. C. (n.d.). *Journal of Writing, 44*(3), 77-88. doi: 10.1234567890

Journal Article, Two Authors, Advance Online Publication, with DOI

Anders, J. C., & Beiler, R. C. (2014). Formatting for beginners. *Journal of Writing,* Advance online publication. doi: 10.1234567890

Journal Article, Two Authors, No Date, Advance Online Publication, with DOI

Anders, J. C., & Beiler, R. C. (n.d.). Formatting for beginners. *Journal of Writing,* Advance online publication. doi: 10.1234567890

Journal Article, Two Authors, no DOI

Anders, J. C., & Beiler, R. C. (2014). Formatting for beginners. *Journal of Writing, 44,* 77-88. Retrieved from http://www.youversustheworld.com

Journal Article, Two Authors, No Date, no DOI

Anders, J. C., & Beiler, R. C. (n.d.). Formatting for beginners. *Journal of Writing, 44,* 77-88. Retrieved from http://www.youversustheworld.com

Journal Article, Two Authors, Arranged by Issue Number, No DOI

Anders, J. C., & Beiler, R. C. (2014). *Journal of Writing, 44*(3), 77-88. Retrieved from http://www.youversustheworld.com

Journal Article, Two Authors, No Date, Arranged by Issue Number, no DOI

Anders, J. C., & Beiler, R. C. (n.d.). *Journal of Writing, 44*(3), 77-88. Retrieved from http://www.youversustheworld.com

Journal Article, Two Authors, Article from Library Database

Anders, J. C., & Beiler, R. C. (2014). Formatting for beginners. *Journal of Writing, 44*, 77-88. Retrieved from http://www.urlofdatabase.com

Journal Article, Two Authors, No Date, Article from Library Database

Anders, J. C., & Beiler, R. C. (n.d.). Formatting for beginners. *Journal of Writing, 44*, 77-88. Retrieved from http://www.urlofdatabase.com

***Note that the APA Manual does not suggest including database information in your reference as database information changes frequently. If you need to include database information, use the url where you found the article that you are citing. In this case, using a DOI is always preferable.

Journal Article, Two Authors, Advance Online Publication, no DOI

Anders, J. C., & Beiler, R. C. (2014). Formatting for beginners. *Journal of Writing,* Advance online publication. Retrieved from http://www.youversustheworld.com

Journal Article, Two Authors, No Date, Advance Online Publication, no DOI

Anders, J. C., & Beiler, R. C. (n.d.). Formatting for beginners. *Journal of Writing,* Advance online publication. Retrieved from http://www.youversustheworld.com

Journal Article, Two Authors, In Press

Anders, J. C., & Beiler, R. C. (in press). Formatting for beginners. *Journal of Writing.* Retrieved from http://www.youversustheworld.com

Journal Abstract as Original Source, Two Authors, no DOI

Anders, J. C., & Beiler, R. C. (2014). Formatting for beginners. *Journal of Writing, 44,* 77-88. Abstract retrieved from http://www.youversustheworld.com

Journal Abstract as Secondary Source, Two Authors, no DOI

Anders, J. C., & Beiler, R. C. (2014). Formatting for beginners. *Journal of Writing, 44,* 77-88. Abstract retrieved from Name of Large Database. (Accenssion No. 123456789)

Journal Article, Two Authors, Translated Into English

Anders, J. C., & Beiler, R. C. (2014). Seja felix [Be happy]. *Bondade E' A Resposta, 6,* 12-18. Retrieved from http://www.youversustheworld.com

Supplemental Material in Journal, Online

Anders, J. C., & Beiler, R. C. (2014). Formatting for beginners [Supplemental material]. *Journal of Writing, 79,* 125-141. http://dx.doi.or/10.1234567890

Journal Article, Two Authors, with Special Issue

Anders, J. C., & Beiler, R. C. (2014). Writing articles in euphoric state [Special issue]. *Righting Writers' Wrongs, 14*(8).

Journal Article, Two Authors, with Special Section

Anders, J. C., & Beiler, R. C. (2014). Writing articles in euphoric state [Special section]. *Righting Writers' Wrongs, 14*(8).

Online Newspaper Article, Two Authors

Anders, J., Beiler, R. (2014). Formatting for beginners. *The Denver Post,* pp. A3, A4. Retrieved from www.denverpost.com

Editorial Online, Two Authors

Anders, J. C., & Beiler, R. C. (2014). Formatting for fun [Editorial]. *Journal of Editing, 6,* 13-15. Retrieved from http://www.youversutheworld.com

Editorial Online, Two Authors, with DOI

Anders, J. C., & Beiler, R. C. (2014). Formatting for fun [Editorial]. *Journal of Editing, 6,* 13-15. doi:10.1234567890

Newsletter, Two Authors

Anders, J. C., & Beiler, R. C. (2014, May/June). Winning is fun. *Corporate Italicized News.* Retrieved from http://www.exacturlifpossible.com/html/news/may/newsletter

Newsletter, Two Authors, Exact Publication Date

Anders, J. C., & Beiler, R. C. (2014, May 6). Winning is fun. *Corporate Italicized News.* Retrieved from http://www.exacturlifpossible.com/html/news/may/newsletter

Newsletter, Two Authors, with DOI

Anders, J. C., & Beiler, R. C. (2014, May/June). Winning is fun. *Corporate Italicized News.* doi: 10.1234567890

Periodicals With Three to Seven Authors

A Quick Overview : **Periodicals with Three to Seven Authors***

Sample Reference Structure

Author Last Name, First Initial., Second Last Name, First Initial., & Third Author Last Name, Third Author First (Year of Publication). Name of article. *Title of Periodical, Periodical number,* Page numbers.

Example:

Anders, J. C., Beiler, R. C., & Zeigler, L. P. (2014). Formatting for beginners. *Journal of Writing, 44,* 77-88.

Electronic Sample

Author Last Name, First Initial., Second Last Name, First Initial., & Third Author Last Name, Third Author First (Year of Publication). Name of article. *Title of Periodical, Periodical number,* Page numbers. doi: xx-xxxxxxxxxx

Electronic Example

Anders, J. C., Beiler, R. C., & Zeigler, L. P. (2014). Formatting for beginners. *Journal of Writing, 44,* 77-88. doi: 10.1234567890

Sample In-Text Citations

For your first time citing a book with three authors, your in text citation should appear like this:
(Smith, Johnson, & Zeigler, 2013)

For subsequent paragraph citation after the first
(Smith et al., 2013)

Every subsequent citation omits the year:
(Smith et al.)

Example #1: Paraphrase
There have been cases where people have compared Smith, Johnson, and Zeigler (2012) to *APA Made Easy* because of the similarities in writing style.

Example #2: Paraphrase

Smith et al. (2012) have compared to APA formatting to MLA formatting.

Example #3: Second Instance of Paraphrase

Smith et al. have compared to APA formatting to MLA formatting.

Example #4: Direct Quote

The book on Fairy Tales was described as "a wonderful tale of hope and dreams" (Smith, Johnson, & Zeigler, 2012, p. 9).

Example #5: Direct Quote, Second Instance

The book on Fairy Tales was described as "a wonderful tale of hope and dreams" (Smith et al., 2012, p. 9).

*Periodicals with three to seven authors will follow the same author's name pattern and in text citation pattern as book references. For example:

Journal with Four Authors:

Anders, J. C., Reilly, B., Beiler, R. C., & Zeigler, L. P. (2014). Formatting for beginners. *Journal of Writing, 44*, 77-88.

In Text Citation:

(Smith, Johnson, Hadden, & Zeigler, 2013)

For subsequent paragraph citation after the first

(Smith et al., 2013)

Every subsequent citation omits the year:

(Smith et al.)

Journal with Five Authors:

Anders, J. C., Havalaand, Q., Reilly, B., Beiler, R. C., & Zeigler, L. P. (2014). Formatting for beginners. *Journal of Writing, 44*, 77-88.

For your first time citing a book with five authors, your in text citation should appear like this:

(Anders, Havalaand, Reilly, Beiler, & Zeigler, 2013)

For subsequent paragraph citation after the first

(Smith et al., 2013)

Every subsequent citation omits the year:

(Smith et al.)

Journal with Six Authors:

Anders, J. C., Havalaand, Q., Reilly, B., Masters, B. B., Beiler, R. C., & Zeigler, L. P. (2014). Formatting for beginners. *Journal of Writing, 44,* 77-88.

In Text Citations:

(*Example #1*: *Paraphrase*

According to Anders et al. (2012), writing in APA format can be easy.

Example #2: *Paraphrase*

With so many resources available, writing in APA format can be easy (Anders et al., 2012).

Example #3: Direct Quote

Anders et al. (2012) stated, "Writing in APA format can be easy" (p. 6).

Example #4: *Direct Quote*

With so many resources available, writing in APA format can be easy (Anders et al., 2012, p. 6).

Journal with Seven Authors:

Anders, J. C., Havalaand, Q., Reilly, B., Masters, B. B., Hovand, C. V., Beiler, R. C., & Zeigler, L. P. (2014). Formatting for beginners. *Journal of Writing, 44,* 77-88.

In Text Citations:

Example #1: Paraphrase

According to Anders et al. (2012), writing in APA format can be easy.

Example #2: Paraphrase

With so many resources available, writing in APA format can be easy (Anders et al., 2012).

Example #3: Direct Quote

Anders et al. (2012) stated, "Writing in APA format can be easy" (p. 8).

Example #4: Direct Quote

With so many resources available, writing in APA format can be easy (Anders et al., 2012, p. 8).

For brevity's sake, I have provided each type of journal entry below with three authors. If you need to reference a journal entry with four to seven authors, simply combine the author examples above along with the type of journal entry below.

Print Periodicals with Three to Seven Authors

Print Periodical, Three to Seven Authors, Arranged by Volume Number

Anders, J. C., Beiler, R. C., & Zeigler, L. P. (2014). Formatting for beginners. *Journal of Writing, 44*, 77-88.

Print Periodical, Three to Seven Authors, No Date, Arranged by Volume Number

Anders, J. C., Beiler, R. C., & Zeigler, L. P. (n.d.). Formatting for beginners. *Journal of Writing, 44*, 77-88.

Print Periodical, Three to Seven Authors, Arranged by Issue Number

Anders, J. C., Beiler, R. C., & Zeigler, L. P. (2014). Formatting for beginners. *Journal of Writing, 44*(3), 77-88.

Print Periodical, Three to Seven Authors, No Date, Arranged by Issue Number

Anders, J. C., Beiler, R. C., & Zeigler, L. P. (n.d.). Formatting for beginners. *Journal of Writing, 44*(3), 77-88.

Print Periodical, Three to Seven Authors, In Press

Anders, J. C., Beiler, R. C., & Zeigler, L. P. (in press). Formatting for beginners. *Journal of Writing, 44,* 77-88.

Print Periodical, Three to Seven Authors, Translated Into English

Anders, J. C., Beiler, R. C., & Zeigler, L. P. (2014). Seja felix [Be happy]. *Bondade E' A Resposta, 6,* 12-18.

Supplemental Material in Journal, Online

Anders, J. C., Beiler, R. C., & Zeigler, L. P. (2014). Formatting for beginners [Supplemental material]. *Journal of Writing, 79,* 125-141. http://dx.doi.or/10.1234567890

Print Periodical, Three to Seven Authors, with Special Issue

Anders, J. C., Beiler, R. C., & Zeigler, L. P. (2014). Writing articles in euphoric state [Special issue]. *Righting Writers' Wrongs, 14*(8).

Print Periodical, Three to Seven Authors, with Special Section

Anders, J. C., Beiler, R. C., & Zeigler, L. P. (2014). Writing articles in euphoric state [Special section]. *Righting Writers' Wrongs, 14*(8).

Editorial, Three to Seven Authors

Anders, J. C., Beiler, R. C., & Zeigler, L. P. (2014). Formatting for fun [Editorial]. *Journal of Editing, 6,* 13-15

Journal Article, Three to Seven Authors, with DOI

Anders, J. C., Beiler, R. C., & Zeigler, L. P. (2014). Formatting for beginners. *Journal of Writing, 44,* 77-88. doi: 10.1234567890

Journal Article, Three to Seven Authors, No Date, with DOI

Anders, J. C., Beiler, R. C., & Zeigler, L. P. (n.d.). Formatting for beginners. *Journal of Writing, 44,* 77-88. doi: 10.1234567890

Journal Article, Three to Seven Authors, Arranged by Issue Number, with DOI

Anders, J. C., Beiler, R. C., & Zeigler, L. P. (2014). *Journal of Writing, 44*(3), 77-88. doi: 10.1234567890

Journal Article, Three to Seven Authors, No Date, Arranged by Issue Number, with DOI

Anders, J. C., Beiler, R. C., & Zeigler, L. P. (n.d.). *Journal of Writing, 44*(3), 77-88. doi: 10.1234567890

Journal Article, Three to Seven Authors, Advance Online Publication

Anders, J. C., Beiler, R. C., & Zeigler, L. P. (n.d.). Formatting for beginners. *Journal of Writing,* Advance online publication. doi: 10.1234567890

Journal Article, Three to Seven Authors, No Date, Advance Online Publication

Anders, J. C., Beiler, R. C., & Zeigler, L. P. (n.d.). Formatting for beginners. *Journal of Writing,* Advance online publication. doi: 10.1234567890

Journal Article, Three to Seven Authors, no DOI

Anders, J. C., Beiler, R. C., & Zeigler, L. P. (2014). Formatting for beginners. *Journal of Writing, 44,* 77-88. Retrieved from http://www.youversustheworld.com

Journal Article, Three to Seven Authors, No Date, no DOI

Anders, J. C., Beiler, R. C., & Zeigler, L. P. (n.d.). Formatting for beginners. *Journal of Writing, 44,* 77-88. Retrieved from http://www.youversustheworld.com

Journal Article, Three to Seven Authors, Arranged by Issue Number, no DOI

Anders, J. C., Beiler, R. C., & Zeigler, L. P. (2014). *Journal of Writing, 44*(3), 77-88. Retrieved from http://www.youversustheworld.com

Journal Article, Three to Seven Authors, No Date, Arranged by Issue Number, no DOI

Anders, J. C., Beiler, R. C., & Zeigler, L. P. (n.d.). *Journal of Writing, 44*(3), 77-88. Retrieved from http://www.youversustheworld.com

Journal Article, Three to Seven Authors, Article from Library Database

Anders, J. C., Beiler, R. C., & Zeigler, L. P. (2014). Formatting for beginners. *Journal of Writing, 44,* 77-88. Retrieved from http://www.urlofdatabase.com

Journal Article, Three to Seven Authors, No Date, Article from Library Database

Anders, J. C., Beiler, R. C., & Zeigler, L. P. (2014). Formatting for beginners. *Journal of Writing, 44,* 77-88. Retrieved from http://www.urlofdatabase.com

***Note that the APA Manual does not suggest including database information in your reference as database information changes frequently. If you need to include database information, use the url where you found the article that you are citing. In this case, using a DOI is always preferable.

Journal Article, Three to Seven Authors, Advance Online Publication, no DOI

Anders, J. C., Beiler, R. C., & Zeigler, L. P. (2014). Formatting for beginners. *Journal of Writing,* Advance online publication. Retrieved from http://www.youversustheworld.com

Journal Article, Three to Seven Authors, No Date, Advance Online Publication, no DOI

Anders, J. C., Beiler, R. C., & Zeigler, L. P. (n.d.). Formatting for beginners. *Journal of Writing,* Advance online publication. Retrieved from http://www.youversustheworld.com

Journal Article, Three to Seven Authors, In Press

Anders, J. C., Beiler, R. C., & Zeigler, L. P. (2014). Formatting for beginners. *Journal of Writing.* Retrieved from http://www.youversustheworld.com

Journal Abstract as Original Source, Three to Seven Authors, no DOI

Anders, J. C., Beiler, R. C., & Zeigler, L. P. (2014). Formatting for beginners. *Journal of Writing, 44,* 77-88. Abstract retrieved from http://www.youversustheworld.com

Journal Abstract as Secondary Source, Three to Seven Authors, no DOI

Anders, J. C., Beiler, R. C., & Zeigler, L. P. (2014). Formatting for beginners. *Journal of Writing, 44,* 77-88. Abstract retrieved from Name of Large Database. (Accession No. 123456789)

Journal Article, Three to Seven Authors, Translated Into English

Anders, J. C., Beiler, R. C., & Zeigler, L. P. (2014). Seja felix [Be happy]. *Bondade E' A Resposta, 6,* 12-18. Retrieved from http://www.youversustheworld.com

Supplemental Material in Journal, Online

Anders, J. C., Beiler, R. C., & Zeigler, L. P. (2014). Formatting for beginners [Supplemental material]. *Journal of Writing, 79,* 125-141. http://dx.doi.or/10.1234567890

Journal Article, Three to Seven Authors, with Special Issue

Anders, J. C., Beiler, R. C., & Zeigler, L. P. (2014). Writing articles in euphoric state [Special issue]. *Righting Writers' Wrongs, 14*(8).

Journal Article, Three to Seven Authors, with Special Section

Anders, J. C., Beiler, R. C., & Zeigler, L. P. (2014). Writing articles in euphoric state [Special section]. *Righting Writers' Wrongs, 14*(8).

Online Newspaper Article, Three to Seven Authors

Anders, J. C., Beiler, R. C., & Zeigler, L. P. (2014). Formatting for beginners. *The Denver Post,* pp. A3, A4. Retrieved from www.denverpost.com

Editorial Online, Three Authors

Anders, J. C., Beiler, R. C., & Zeigler, L. P. (2014). Formatting for fun [Editorial]. *Journal of Editing, 6,* 13-15. Retrieved from http://www.youversutheworld.com

Editorial Online, Three Authors, with DOI

Anders, J. C., Beiler, R. C., & Zeigler, L. P. (2014). Formatting for fun [Editorial]. *Journal of Editing, 6,* 13-15. doi:10.1234567890

Newsletter, Three authors

Anders, J. C., Beiler, R. C., & Zeigler, L. P. (2014, May/June). Winning is fun. *Corporate Italicized News.* Retrieved from http://www.exacturlifpossible.com/html/news/may/newsletter

Newsletter, Three authors, Exact Publication Date

Anders, J. C., Beiler, R. C., & Zeigler, L. P. (2014, May 6). Winning is fun. *Corporate Italicized News.* Retrieved from http://www.exacturlifpossible.com/html/news/may/newsletter

Newsletter, Three authors, with DOI

Anders, J. C., Beiler, R. C., & Zeigler, L. P. (2014, May/June). Winning is fun. *Corporate Italicized News.* doi:10.1234567890

Periodicals With Seven or More Authors

A Quick Overview : ***Periodicals with More than Seven Authors***

Sample Reference Structure

Last Name, First Initial., Second Last Name, First Initial., Third Last Name, Third First Initial., Fifth Last Name, Fifth First Initial., Sixth Last Name, Sixth First Initial., . . . Eighth/Final Last Name, Eighth/Final First Initial. (Date of Publication). Name of article. *Title of Periodical, Periodical number,* Page numbers.

Example:

Anders, J. C., Havalaand, Q., Peters, B. W., Reilly, B., Masters, B. B., Hovand, C. V., Beiler, R. C., & Zeigler, L. P. (2014). Formatting for beginners. *Journal of Writing, 44,* 77-88.

Electronic Sample

Last Name, First Initial., Second Last Name, First Initial., Third Last Name, Third First Initial., Fifth Last Name, Fifth First Initial., Sixth Last Name, Sixth First Initial., . . . Eighth/Final Last Name, Eighth/Final First Initial. (Date of Publication). Name of article. *Title of Periodical, Periodical number,* Page numbers. doi: xx-xxxxxxxxxx

Electronic Example

Anders, J. C., Havalaand, Q., Peters, B. W., Reilly, B., Masters, B. B., Hovand, C. V., Beiler, R. C., & Zeigler, L. P. (2014). Formatting for beginners. *Journal of Writing, 44,* 77-88. doi: 10.1234567890

Sample In-Text Citations

Example #1: Paraphrase

According to Anders et al. (2012), writing in APA format can be easy.

Example #2: Paraphrase

With so many resources available, writing in APA format can be easy (Anders et al., 2012).

Example #3: Direct Quote

Anders et al. (2012) stated, "Writing in APA format can be easy" (p. iv).

Example #4: Direct Quote

With so many resources available, writing in APA format can be easy (Anders et al., 2012, p. 16).

Periodicals with More Than Seven Authors

Print Periodical, More Than Seven Authors, Arranged by Volume Number

Creston, J. P., Anders, R. F., Wilson, D. A., Peters, B. O., Roberts, M. A., Mathers, Y. O., . . . Nehman, T. (2014). Formatting for beginners. *Journal of Writing, 44,* 77-88.

Print Periodical, More Than Seven Authors, No Date, Arranged by Volume Number

Creston, J. P., Anders, R. F., Wilson, D. A., Peters, B. O., Roberts, M. A., Mathers, Y. O., . . . Nehman, T. (n.d.). Formatting for beginners. *Journal of Writing, 44,* 77-88.

Print Periodical, More Than Seven Authors, Arranged by Issue Number

Creston, J. P., Anders, R. F., Wilson, D. A., Peters, B. O., Roberts, M. A., Mathers, Y. O., . . . Nehman, T. (2014). Formatting for beginners. *Journal of Writing, 44*(3), 77-88.

Print Periodical, More Than Seven Authors, No Date, Arranged by Issue Number

Creston, J. P., Anders, R. F., Wilson, D. A., Peters, B. O., Roberts, M. A., Mathers, Y. O., . . . Nehman, T. (n.d.). Formatting for beginners. *Journal of Writing, 44*(3), 77-88.

Print Periodical, More than Seven Authors, In Press

Creston, J. P., Anders, R. F., Wilson, D. A., Peters, B. O., Roberts, M. A., Mathers, Y. O., . . . Nehman, T. (in press). Formatting for beginners. *Journal of Writing, 44,* 77-88.

Print Periodical, More than Seven Authors, Translated Into English

Creston, J. P., Anders, R. F., Wilson, D. A., Peters, B. O., Roberts, M. A., Mathers, Y. O., . . . Nehman, T. (2014). Seja felix [Be happy]. *Bondade E' A Resposta, 6,* 12-18.

Supplemental Material in Journal, Online

Creston, J. P., Anders, R. F., Wilson, D. A., Peters, B. O., Roberts, M. A., Mathers, Y. O., . . . Nehman, T. (2014). Formatting for beginners [Supplemental material]. *Journal of Writing, 79,* 125-141. http://dx.doi.or/10.1234567890

Print Periodical, More than Seven Authors, with Special Issue

Creston, J. P., Anders, R. F., Wilson, D. A., Peters, B. O., Roberts, M. A., Mathers, Y. O., . . . Nehman, T. (2014). Writing articles in euphoric state [Special issue]. *Righting Writers' Wrongs, 14*(8).

Print Periodical, More than Seven Authors, with Special Section

Creston, J. P., Anders, R. F., Wilson, D. A., Peters, B. O., Roberts, M. A., Mathers, Y. O., . . . Nehman, T. (2014). Writing articles in euphoric state [Special section]. *Righting Writers' Wrongs, 14*(8).

Journal Article, More Than Seven Authors, With DOI

Creston, J. P., Anders, R. F., Wilson, D. A., Peters, B. O., Roberts, M. A., Mathers, Y. O., . . . Nehman, T. (2014). Formatting for beginners. *Journal of Writing, 44,* 77-88. doi: 10.1234567890

Journal Article, More Than Seven Authors, No Date, With DOI

Creston, J. P., Anders, R. F., Wilson, D. A., Peters, B. O., Roberts, M. A., Mathers, Y. O., . . . Nehman, T. (n.d.). Formatting for beginners. *Journal of Writing, 44,* 77-88. doi: 10.1234567890

Journal Article, More Than Seven Authors, Arranged by Issue Number, with DOI

Creston, J. P., Anders, R. F., Wilson, D. A., Peters, B. O., Roberts, M. A., Mathers, Y. O., . . . Nehman, T. (2014). *Journal of Writing, 44*(3), 77-88. doi: 10.1234567890

Journal Article, More Than Seven Authors, No Date, Arranged by Issue Number, with DOI

Creston, J. P., Anders, R. F., Wilson, D. A., Peters, B. O., Roberts, M. A., Mathers, Y. O., . . . Nehman, T. (n.d.). *Journal of Writing, 44*(3), 77-88. doi: 10.1234567890

Journal Article, More Than Seven Authors, Advance Online Publication with DOI

Creston, J. P., Anders, R. F., Wilson, D. A., Peters, B. O., Roberts, M. A., Mathers, Y. O., . . . Nehman, T. (2014). Formatting for beginners. *Journal of Writing,* Advance online publication. doi: 10.1234567890

Journal Article, More Than Seven Authors, No Date, Advance Online Publication with DOI

Creston, J. P., Anders, R. F., Wilson, D. A., Peters, B. O., Roberts, M. A., Mathers, Y. O., . . . Nehman, T. (n.d.). Formatting for beginners. *Journal of Writing,* Advance online publication. doi: 10.1234567890

Journal Article, More than Seven Authors, no DOI

Creston, J. P., Anders, R. F., Wilson, D. A., Peters, B. O., Roberts, M. A., Mathers, Y. O., . . . Nehman, T. (2014). Formatting for beginners. *Journal of Writing, 44,* 77-88. Retrieved from http://www.youversustheworld.com

Journal Article, More than Seven Authors, No Date, no DOI

Creston, J. P., Anders, R. F., Wilson, D. A., Peters, B. O., Roberts, M. A., Mathers, Y. O., . . . Nehman, T. (n.d.). Formatting for beginners. *Journal of Writing, 44,* 77-88. Retrieved from http://www.youversustheworld.com

Journal Article, More than Seven Authors, Arranged by Issue Number, no DOI

Creston, J. P., Anders, R. F., Wilson, D. A., Peters, B. O., Roberts, M. A., Mathers, Y. O., . . . Nehman, T. (2014). Formatting for beginners. *Journal of Writing, 44*(3), 77-88. Retrieved from http://www.youversustheworld.com

Journal Article, More than Seven Authors, No Date, Arranged by Issue Number, no DOI

Creston, J. P., Anders, R. F., Wilson, D. A., Peters, B. O., Roberts, M. A., Mathers, Y. O., . . . Nehman, T. (n.d.). Formatting for beginners. *Journal of Writing, 44*(3), 77-88. Retrieved from http://www.youversustheworld.com

Journal Article, More Than Seven Authors, Article from Library Database

Creston, J. P., Anders, R. F., Wilson, D. A., Peters, B. O., Roberts, M. A., Mathers, Y. O., . . . Nehman, T. (2014). Formatting for beginners. *Journal of Writing, 44,* 77-88. Retrieved from http://www.urlofdatabase.com

Journal Article, More Than Seven Authors, No Date, Article from Library Database

Creston, J. P., Anders, R. F., Wilson, D. A., Peters, B. O., Roberts, M. A., Mathers, Y. O., . . . Nehman, T. (2014). Formatting for beginners. *Journal of Writing, 44,* 77-88. Retrieved from http://www.urlofdatabase.com

***Note that the APA Manual does not suggest including database information in your reference as database information changes frequently. If you need to include database information, use the url where you found the article that you are citing. In this case, using a DOI is always preferable.

Journal Article, More Than Seven Authors, Advance Online Publication no DOI

Creston, J. P., Anders, R. F., Wilson, D. A., Peters, B. O., Roberts, M. A., Mathers, Y. O., . . . Nehman, T. (2014). Formatting for beginners. *Journal of Writing,* Advance online publication. Retrieved from http://www.youversustheworld.com

Journal Article, More Than Seven Authors, No Date, Advance Online Publication no DOI

Creston, J. P., Anders, R. F., Wilson, D. A., Peters, B. O., Roberts, M. A., Mathers, Y. O., . . . Nehman, T. (n.d.). Formatting for beginners. *Journal of Writing,* Advance online publication. Retrieved from http://www.youversustheworld.com

Journal Article, More than Seven Authors, In Press

Creston, J. P., Anders, R. F., Wilson, D. A., Peters, B. O., Roberts, M. A., Mathers, Y. O., . . . Nehman, T. (in press). Formatting for beginners. *Journal of Writing*. Retrieved from http://www.youversustheworld.com

Journal Abstract as Original Source, More than Seven Authors, no DOI

Creston, J. P., Anders, R. F., Wilson, D. A., Peters, B. O., Roberts, M. A., Mathers, Y. O., . . . Nehman, T. (2014). Formatting for beginners. *Journal of Writing, 44,* 77-88. Abstract retrieved from http://www.youversustheworld.com

Journal Abstract as Secondary Source, More than Seven Authors, no DOI

Creston, J. P., Anders, R. F., Wilson, D. A., Peters, B. O., Roberts, M. A., Mathers, Y. O., . . . Nehman, T. (2014). Formatting for beginners. *Journal of Writing, 44,* 77-88. Abstract retrieved from Name of Large Database. (Accenssion No. 123456789)

Journal Article, More than Seven Authors, Translated Into English

Creston, J. P., Anders, R. F., Wilson, D. A., Peters, B. O., Roberts, M. A., Mathers, Y. O., . . . Nehman, T. (2014). Seja felix [Be happy]. *Bondade E' A Resposta, 6,* 12-18. Retrieved from http://www.youversustheworld.com

Supplemental Material in Journal, Online

Creston, J. P., Anders, R. F., Wilson, D. A., Peters, B. O., Roberts, M. A., Mathers, Y. O., . . . Nehman, T. (2014). Formatting for beginners [Supplemental material]. *Journal of Writing, 79,* 125-141. http://dx.doi.or/10.1234567890

Journal Article, More than Seven Authors, with Special Issue

Creston, J. P., Anders, R. F., Wilson, D. A., Peters, B. O., Roberts, M. A., Mathers, Y. O., . . . Nehman, T. (2014). Writing articles in euphoric state [Special issue]. *Righting Writers' Wrongs, 14*(8).

Journal Article, More than Seven Authors, with Special Section

Creston, J. P., Anders, R. F., Wilson, D. A., Peters, B. O., Roberts, M. A., Mathers, Y. O., . . . Nehman, T. (2014). Writing articles in euphoric state [Special section]. *Righting Writers' Wrongs, 14*(8).

Magazine Articles

A Quick Overview : **Magazine Articles**

General Template:

Author Last Name, First Initial. Middle Initial. (Year, Month of Publication). Name of article. *Name of Publication, Volume number,* Page numbers.

Example:

Anders, J. C. (2014, May). Writing perfect papers. *Formatting Monthly Magazine, 17,* 32-34.

Magazine Articles follow the same formatting as the periodicals above.

- *In text citations for Magazines without an author, see page 147*
- *In text citations for Magazines with one author, see page 154*
- *In text citations for Magazines with two authors, see page 161*
- *In text citations for Magazines with two authors, see page 168*

Magazine Articles

Print Magazine Article, No Author

Writing perfect papers. (2014, May). *Formatting Monthly Magazine, 17,* 32-34.

Print Magazine Article, No Author, No Date

Writing perfect papers. (n.d.). *Formatting Monthly Magazine, 17,* 32-34.

Print Magazine Article, No Author, with weekly or daily date

Writing perfect papers. (2014, May 6). *Formatting Monthly Magazine, 17,* 32-34.

Print Magazine Article, No Author, Arranged by Issue Number

Writing perfect papers. (2014, May). *Formatting Monthly Magazine, 17*(3), 32-34.

Print Magazine Article, No Author, No Date, Arranged by Issue Number

Writing perfect papers. (n.d.). *Formatting Monthly Magazine, 17*(3), 32-34.

Online Magazine Article, No Author

Writing perfect papers. (2014, May). *Formatting Monthly Magazine, 17,* 32-34. Retrieved from http://www.youversustheworld.com

Online Magazine Article, No Author, No Date

Writing perfect papers. (n.d.). *Formatting Monthly Magazine, 17,* 32-34. Retrieved from http://www.youversustheworld.com

Online Magazine Article, No Author, with weekly or daily date

Writing perfect papers. (2014, May 6). *Formatting Monthly Magazine, 17,* 32-34. Retrieved from http://www.youversustheworld.com

Online Magazine Article, No Author, Arranged by Issue Number

Writing perfect papers. (2014, May). *Formatting Monthly Magazine, 17*(3), 32-34. Retrieved from http://www.youversustheworld.com

Online Magazine Article, No Author, No Date, Arranged by Issue Number

Writing perfect papers. (n.d.). *Formatting Monthly Magazine, 17*(3), 32-34. Retrieved from http://www.youversustheworld.com

Journal Article, No Author, Found in Library Database

Formatting for beginners. (2014). *Journal of Writing, 44,* 77-88. Retrieved from www.urlofdatabase.edu

Online Magazine Article, No Author, No Date, Found in Library Database

Formatting for beginners. (n.d.). *Journal of Writing, 44,* 77-88. Retrieved from www.urlofdatabase.edu

***Note that the APA Manual does not suggest including database information in your reference as database information changes frequently. If you need to include database information, use the url where you found the article that you are citing. In this case, using a DOI is always preferable.

Online Magazine Article, No Author, with DOI

Writing perfect papers. (2014, May). *Formatting Monthly Magazine, 17,* 32-34. doi: 10.1234567890

Online Magazine Article, No Author, No Date, with DOI

Writing perfect papers. (n.d.). *Formatting Monthly Magazine, 17,* 32-34. doi: 10.1234567890

Online Magazine Article, No Author, Arranged by Issue Number, with DOI

Writing perfect papers. (2014, May). *Formatting Monthly Magazine, 17*(3), 32-34. doi: 10.1234567890

Online Magazine Article, No Author, No Date, Arranged by Issue Number, with DOI

Writing perfect papers. (n.d.). *Formatting Monthly Magazine, 17*(3), 32-34. doi: 10.1234567890

Magazine Articles with One Author

Print Magazine Article, One Author

Anders, J. C. (2014, May). Writing perfect papers. *Formatting Monthly Magazine, 17*, 32-34.

Print Magazine Article, One Author, No Date

Anders, J. C. (n.d.). Writing perfect papers. *Formatting Monthly Magazine, 17*, 32-34.

Print Magazine Article, One Author, with weekly or daily date

Anders, J. C. (2014, May 6). Writing perfect papers. *Formatting Monthly Magazine, 17*, 32-34.

Print Magazine Article, One Author, Arranged by Issue Number

Anders, J. C. (2014, May). Writing perfect papers. *Formatting Monthly Magazine, 17*(3), 32-34.

Print Magazine Article, One Author, No Date, Arranged by Issue Number

Anders, J. C. (n.d.). Writing perfect papers. *Formatting Monthly Magazine, 17*(3), 32-34.

Online Magazine Article, One Author

Anders, J. C. (2014, May). Writing perfect papers. *Formatting Monthly Magazine, 17*, 32-34. Retrieved from http://www.youversustheworld.com

Online Magazine Article, One Author, No Date

Anders, J. C. (n.d.). Writing perfect papers. *Formatting Monthly Magazine, 17*, 32-34. Retrieved from http://www.youversustheworld.com

Online Magazine Article, One Author, with weekly or daily date

Anders, J. C. (2014, May 6). Writing perfect papers. *Formatting Monthly Magazine, 17*, 32-34. Retrieved from http://www.youversustheworld.com

Online Magazine Article, One Author, Arranged by Issue Number

Anders, J. C. (2014, May). Writing perfect papers. *Formatting Monthly Magazine, 17*(3), 32-34. Retrieved from http://www.youversustheworld.com

Online Magazine Article, One Author, No Date, Arranged by Issue Number

Anders, J. C. (n.d.). Writing perfect papers. *Formatting Monthly Magazine, 17*(3), 32-34. Retrieved from http://www.youversustheworld.com

Online Magazine Article, One Author, Found in Library Database

Anders, J. C. (2014). Formatting for beginners. *Journal of Writing, 44,* 77-88. Retrieved from www.urlofdatabase.edu

Online Magazine Article, One Author, No Date, Found in Library Database

Anders, J. C. (n.d.). Formatting for beginners. *Journal of Writing, 44,* 77-88. Retrieved from www.urlofdatabase.edu

***Note that the APA Manual does not suggest including database information in your reference as database information changes frequently. If you need to include database information, use the url where you found the article that you are citing. In this case, using a DOI is always preferable.

Online Magazine Article, One Author, with DOI

Anders, J. C. (2014, May). Writing perfect papers. *Formatting Monthly Magazine, 17,* 32-34. doi: 10.1234567890

Online Magazine Article, One Author, No Date, with DOI

Anders, J. C. (n.d.). Writing perfect papers. *Formatting Monthly Magazine, 17,* 32-34. doi: 10.1234567890

Online Magazine Article, One Author, Arranged by Issue Number, with DOI

Anders, J. C. (2014, May). Writing perfect papers. *Formatting Monthly Magazine, 17*(3), 32-34. doi:10.1234567890

Online Magazine Article, One Author, No Date, Arranged by Issue Number, with DOI

Anders, J. C. (n.d.). Writing perfect papers. *Formatting Monthly Magazine, 17*(3), 32-34. doi: 10.1234567890

Magazine Article with Two Authors

Print Magazine Article, Two Authors

Anders, J. C. & Beiler, R. C. (2014, May). Writing perfect papers. *Formatting Monthly Magazine, 17,* 32-34.

Print Magazine Article, Two Authors, No Date

Anders, J. C. & Beiler, R. C. (n.d.). Writing perfect papers. *Formatting Monthly Magazine, 17,* 32-34.

Print Magazine Article, Two Authors, with weekly or daily date

Anders, J. C. & Beiler, R. C. (2014, May 6). Writing perfect papers. *Formatting Monthly Magazine, 17,* 32-34.

Print Magazine Article, Two Authors, Arranged by Issue Number

Anders, J. C. & Beiler, R. C. (2014, May). Writing perfect papers. *Formatting Monthly Magazine, 17*(3), 32-34.

Print Magazine Article, Two Authors, No Date, Arranged by Issue Number

Anders, J. C. & Beiler, R. C. (n.d.). Writing perfect papers. *Formatting Monthly Magazine, 17*(3), 32-34.

Online Magazine Article, Two Authors

Anders, J. C. & Beiler, R. C. (2014, May). Writing perfect papers. *Formatting Monthly Magazine, 17,* 32-34. Retrieved from http://www.youversustheworld.com

Online Magazine Article, Two Authors, No Date

Anders, J. C. & Beiler, R. C. (n.d.). Writing perfect papers. *Formatting Monthly Magazine, 17,* 32-34. Retrieved from http://www.youversustheworld.com

Online Magazine Article, Two Authors, with weekly or daily date

Anders, J. C. & Beiler, R. C. (2014, May 6). Writing perfect papers. *Formatting Monthly Magazine, 17,* 32-34. Retrieved from http://www.youversustheworld.com

Online Magazine Article, Two Authors, Arranged by Issue Number

Anders, J. C. & Beiler, R. C. (2014, May). Writing perfect papers. *Formatting Monthly Magazine, 17*(3), 32-34. Retrieved from http://www.youversustheworld.com

Online Magazine Article, Two Authors, No Date, Arranged by Issue Number

Anders, J. C. & Beiler, R. C. (n.d.). Writing perfect papers. *Formatting Monthly Magazine, 17*(3), 32-34. Retrieved from http://www.youversustheworld.com

Online Magazine Article, Two Authors, Found in Library Database

Anders, J. C. & Beiler, R. C. (2014). Formatting for beginners. *Journal of Writing, 44,* 77-88. Retrieved from www.urlofdatabase.edu

Online Magazine Article, Two Authors, No Date, Found in Library Database

Anders, J. C. & Beiler, R. C. (n.d.). Formatting for beginners. *Journal of Writing, 44,* 77-88. Retrieved from www.urlofdatabase.edu

***Note that the APA Manual does not suggest including database information in your reference as database information changes frequently. If you need to include database information, use the url where you found the article that you are citing. In this case, using a DOI is always preferable.

Online Magazine Article, Two Authors, with DOI

Anders, J. C. & Beiler, R. C. (2014, May). Writing perfect papers. *Formatting Monthly Magazine, 17,* 32-34. doi:10.1234567890

Online Magazine Article, Two Authors, No Date, with DOI

Anders, J. C. & Beiler, R. C. (n.d.). Writing perfect papers. *Formatting Monthly Magazine, 17,* 32-34. doi:10.1234567890

Online Magazine Article, Two Authors, Arranged by Issue Number, with DOI

Anders, J. C. & Beiler, R. C. (2014, May). Writing perfect papers. *Formatting Monthly Magazine, 17*(3), 32-34. doi:10.1234567890

Online Magazine Article, Two Authors, No Date, Arranged by Issue Number, with DOI

Anders, J. C. & Beiler, R. C. (n.d.). Writing perfect papers. *Formatting Monthly Magazine, 17*(3), 32-34. doi:10.1234567890

Print Magazine Article with Three Authors

Print Magazine Article, Three Authors

Anders, J. C., Beiler, R. C., & Zeigler, L. P. (2014, May). Writing perfect papers. *Formatting Monthly Magazine, 17,* 32-34.

Print Magazine Article, Three Authors, No Date

Anders, J. C., Beiler, R. C., & Zeigler, L. P. (n.d.). Writing perfect papers. *Formatting Monthly Magazine, 17,* 32-34.

Print Magazine Article, Three Authors, with weekly or daily date

Anders, J. C., Beiler, R. C., & Zeigler, L. P. (2014, May 6). Writing perfect papers. *Formatting Monthly Magazine, 17,* 32-34.

Print Magazine Article, Three Authors, Arranged by Issue Number

Anders, J. C., Beiler, R. C., & Zeigler, L. P. (2014, May). Writing perfect papers. *Formatting Monthly Magazine, 17*(3), 32-34.

Print Magazine Article, Three Authors, No Date, Arranged by Issue Number

Anders, J. C., Beiler, R. C., & Zeigler, L. P. (n.d.). Writing perfect papers. *Formatting Monthly Magazine, 17*(3), 32-34.

Online Magazine Article, Three Authors

Anders, J. C., Beiler, R. C., & Zeigler, L. P. (2014, May). Writing perfect papers. *Formatting Monthly Magazine, 17,* 32-34. Retrieved from http://www.youversustheworld.com

Online Magazine Article, Three Authors, No Date

Anders, J. C., Beiler, R. C., & Zeigler, L. P. (n.d.). Writing perfect papers. *Formatting Monthly Magazine, 17,* 32-34. Retrieved from http://www.youversustheworld.com

Online Magazine Article, Three Authors, with Weekly or Daily Date

Anders, J. C., Beiler, R. C., & Zeigler, L. P. (2014, May). Writing perfect papers. *Formatting Monthly Magazine, 17,* 32-34. Retrieved from http://www.youversustheworld.com

Online Magazine Article, Three Authors, Arranged by Issue Number

Anders, J. C., Beiler, R. C., & Zeigler, L. P. (2014, May). Writing perfect papers. *Formatting Monthly Magazine, 17*(3), 32-34. Retrieved from http://www.youversustheworld.com

Online Magazine Article, Three Authors, No Date, Arranged by Issue Number

Anders, J. C., Beiler, R. C., & Zeigler, L. P. (n.d.). Writing perfect papers. *Formatting Monthly Magazine, 17*(3), 32-34. Retrieved from http://www.youversustheworld.com

Online Magazine Article, Three Authors, Found in Library Database

Anders, J. C., Beiler, R. C., & Zeigler, L. P. (2014). Formatting for beginners. *Journal of Writing, 44,* 77-88. Retrieved from www.urlofdatabase.edu

Online Magazine Article, Three Authors, No Date, Found in Library Database

Anders, J. C., Beiler, R. C., & Zeigler, L. P. (n.d.). Formatting for beginners. *Journal of Writing, 44,* 77-88. Retrieved from www.urlofdatabase.edu

***Note that the APA Manual does not suggest including database information in your reference as database information changes frequently. If you need to include database information, use the url where you found the article that you are citing. In this case, using a DOI is always preferable.

Online Magazine Article, Three Authors, with DOI

Anders, J. C., Beiler, R. C., & Zeigler, L. P. (2014, May). Writing perfect papers. *Formatting Monthly Magazine, 17,* 32-34. doi:10.1234567890

Online Magazine Article, Three Authors, No Date, with DOI

Anders, J. C., Beiler, R. C., & Zeigler, L. P. (n.d.). Writing perfect papers. *Formatting Monthly Magazine, 17,* 32-34. doi:10.1234567890

Online Magazine Article, Three Authors, Arranged by Issue Number, with DOI

Anders, J. C., Beiler, R. C., & Zeigler, L. P. (2014, May). Writing perfect papers. *Formatting Monthly Magazine, 17*(3), 32-34. doi:10.1234567890

Online Magazine Article, Three Authors, No Date, Arranged by Issue Number, with DOI

Anders, J. C., Beiler, R. C., & Zeigler, L. P. (n.d.). Writing perfect papers. *Formatting Monthly Magazine, 17*(3), 32-34. doi:10.1234567890

Letter the the Editor

Anders, J. C. (2014, May). Writing perfect papers [Letter to the editor]. *Formatting Monthly Magazine, 17,* 32-34.

Chapter 3 - References for Reviews and Peer Commentary

References for Reviews

A Quick Overview : **Reviews of Books**

General Template

Last name of reviewer, First Initial. Middle Initial. (year). Title of review [Review of the book *Title of medium,* by Author First Initial. Author Middle Initial. Author Last Name]. *Title of work, Volume Number,* page numbers.

Example:

Anders, J. C. (2014). Writing perfect papers. [Review of the book *The hardest paper ever written,* by B. C. Bentley]. *Formatting Monthly Magazine, 17,* 32-34.

In text citations for Reviews follows the same format as the in text citations as books. For in text citation formatting:

- For Reviews with one author, see page 55
- For Reviews with two authors, see page 65
- For Reviews with three authors, see page 76

Review of a Books

Print Review of a Book, One Author

Anders, J. C. (2014). Writing perfect papers. [Review of the book *The hardest paper ever written,* by B. C. Bentley]. *Formatting Monthly Magazine, 17,* 32-34.

Print Review of a Book, One Author, with Index Number

Anders, J. C. (2014). Writing perfect papers. [Review of the book *The hardest paper ever written,* by B. C. Bentley]. *Formatting Monthly Magazine, 17*(4), 32-34.

Print Review of a Book with 2 Authors

Anders, J. C. (2014). Writing perfect papers. [Review of the book *The hardest paper ever written,* by B. C. Bentley & R. C. Cunningham]. *Formatting Monthly Magazine, 17,* 32-34.

Review of an Online Book, no DOI

Anders, J. C. (2014). Writing perfect papers. [Review of the book *The hardest paper ever written,* by B. C. Bentley]. *Formatting Monthly Magazine, 17,* 32-34. Retrieved from http://www.youversustheworld.com

Untitled Review of a Book

Anders, J. C. (2014). [Review of the book *The hardest paper ever written,* by B. C. Bentley]. *Formatting Monthly Magazine, 17,* 32-34.

Print Review of an Online Book with DOI

Anders, J. C. (2014). Writing perfect papers. [Review of the book *The hardest paper ever written,* by B. C. Bentley]. *Formatting Monthly Magazine, 17,* 32-34. doi: 10:1234567890

A Quick Overview : **Reviews of Articles**

General Template

Last name of reviewer, First Initial. Middle Initial. (year). Title of review [Review of the article "Title of article," by Author First Initial. Author Middle Initial. Author Last Name]. *Title of work, Volume Number,* page numbers.

Example:

Anders, J. C. (2014). Writing perfect papers. [Review of the article *The hardest paper ever written,* by B. C. Bentley]. *Formatting Monthly Magazine, 17,* 32-34.

In text citations for Reviews follows the same format as the in text citations as books. For in text citation formatting:

- For Reviews with one author, see page 55
- For Reviews with two authors, see page 65
- For Reviews with three authors, see page 76

Review of an Article

Review of an Article, One Author

Anders, J. C. (2014). Writing perfect papers. [Review of the article "The hardest paper ever written," by B. C. Bentley]. *Formatting Monthly Magazine, 17,* 32-34.

Review of an Article, One Author, with Index Number

Anders, J. C. (2014). Writing perfect papers. [Review of the article "The hardest paper ever written," by B. C. Bentley]. *Formatting Monthly Magazine, 17*(3), 32-34.

Review of an Article, Two Authors

Anders, J. C. (2014). Writing perfect papers. [Review of the article "The hardest paper ever written," by B. C. Bentley & R. C. Cunningham]. *Formatting Monthly Magazine, 17,* 32-34.

Review of an Online Article

Anders, J. C. (2014). Writing perfect papers. [Review of the article "The hardest paper ever written," by B. C. Bentley]. *Formatting Monthly Magazine, 17,* 32-34. Retrieved from http://www.youversustheworld.com

Untitled Review of an Article

Anders, J. C. (2014). [Review of the article *The hardest paper ever written*, by B. C. Bentley]. *Formatting Monthly Magazine, 17,* 32-34.

Untitled Review of an Article Online

Anders, J. C. (2014). [Review of the article *The hardest paper ever written*, by B. C. Bentley]. *Formatting Monthly Magazine, 17,* 32-34. doi:10:1234567890

Review of an Online Article with DOI

Anders, J. C. (2014). Writing perfect papers. [Review of the article "The hardest paper ever written," by B. C. Bentley]. *Formatting Monthly Magazine, 17,* 32-34. doi: 10:1234567890

A Quick Overview : **Reviews of Videos**

General Template

Last name of reviewer, First Initial. Middle Initial. (year). Title of review [Review of the DVD *Title of dvd,* produced by Author First Initial. Author Middle Initial. Author Last Name, Year of Release]. *Title of work, Volume Number,* page numbers.

Example:

Anders, J. C. (2014). Writing perfect papers. [Review of the DVD *The hardest paper ever written,* produced by B. C. Bentley, 2014]. *Formatting Monthly Magazine, 17,* 32-34.

In text citations for Reviews follows the same format as the in text citations as books. For in text citation formatting:

- For Reviews with one author, see page 55
- For Reviews with two authors, see page 65
- For Reviews with three authors, see page 76

Reviews of a Video

Review of a Video, One Author

Anders, J. C. (2014). Writing perfect papers. [Review of the DVD *The hardest paper ever written,* produced by B. C. Bentley, 2014]. *Formatting Monthly Magazine, 17,* 32-34.

Review of a Video, One Author, with Index Number

Anders, J. C. (2014). Writing perfect papers. [Review of the DVD *The hardest paper ever written,* produced by B. C. Bentley, 2014]. *Formatting Monthly Magazine, 17*(1), 32-34.

Review of a Video, no Date

Anders, J. C. (n.d.). Writing perfect papers. [Review of the DVD *The hardest paper ever written,* produced by B. C. Bentley, 2014]. *Formatting Monthly Magazine, 17,* 32-34.

Review of a Video, No Author, with Index Number

[Review of the DVD *The hardest paper ever written,* produced by B. C. Bentley, 2014]. (2014). Writing perfect papers. *Formatting Monthly Magazine, 17*(1), 32-34.

Online Review of a Video

Anders, J. C. (2014). Writing perfect papers. [Review of the DVD *The hardest paper ever written,* produced by B. C. Bentley, 2014]. *Formatting Monthly Magazine, 17,* 32-34. Retrieved from www.youversustheworld.com

Online Review of a Video with DOI

Anders, J. C. (2014). Writing perfect papers. [Review of the DVD *The hardest paper ever written,* produced by B. C. Bentley, 2014]. *Formatting Monthly Magazine, 17,* 32-34. doi: 10.1234567890

Online Review of a Video, No Title, with Index Number

Anders, J. C. (2014). [Review of the DVD *The hardest paper ever written,* produced by B. C. Bentley, 2014]. *Formatting Monthly Magazine, 17*(1), 32-34. doi: 10.1234567890

A Quick Overview : **Reviews of Television Broadcast**

General Template

Last name of reviewer, First Initial. Middle Initial. (year). Title of review [Review of the television broadcast *Title of broadcast,* produced by Author First Initial. Author Middle Initial. Author Last Name, Year of Release]. *Title of work, Volume Number,* page numbers.

Example:

Anders, J. C. (2014). Writing perfect papers. [Review of the television broadcast *The hardest paper ever written,* produced by B. C. Bentley, 2014]. *Formatting Monthly Magazine, 17*(1), 32-34.

In text citations for Reviews follows the same format as the in text citations as books. For in text citation formatting:

- For Reviews with one author, see page 55
- For Reviews with two authors, see page 65
- For Reviews with three authors, see page 76

Reviews of a Television Broadcasts

Review of a Television Broadcast, One Author

Anders, J. C. (2014). Writing perfect papers. [Review of the television broadcast *The hardest paper ever written,* produced by B. C. Bentley, 2014]. *Formatting Monthly Magazine, 17*(1), 32-34.

Review of a Television Broadcast, One Author, with Index Number

Anders, J. C. (2014). Writing perfect papers. [Review of the television broadcast *The hardest paper ever written,* produced by B. C. Bentley, 2014]. *Formatting Monthly Magazine, 17*(1), 32-34.

Review of a Television Broadcast, no Date

Anders, J. C. (n.d.). Writing perfect papers. [Review of the television broadcast *The hardest paper ever written,* produced by B. C. Bentley, 2014]. *Formatting Monthly Magazine, 17,* 32-34.

Review of a Television Broadcast, No Author

[Review of the television broadcast *The hardest paper ever written,* produced by B. C. Bentley, 2014]. (2014). Writing perfect papers. *Formatting Monthly Magazine, 17,* 32-34.

Online Review of a Television Broadcast with DOI

Anders, J. C. (2014). Writing perfect papers. [Review of the television broadcast *The hardest paper ever written,* produced by B. C. Bentley, 2014]. *Formatting Monthly Magazine, 17,* 32-34. doi: 10.1234567890

Online Review of a Television Broadcast, no DOI

Anders, J. C. (2014). Writing perfect papers. [Review of the television broadcast *The hardest paper ever written,* produced by B. C. Bentley, 2014]. *Formatting Monthly Magazine,17,* 32-34. Retrieved from www.youversustheworld.com

Online Review of a Television Broadcast, No Title, with Index Number

Anders, J. C. (2014). [Review of the television broadcast *The hardest paper ever written,* produced by B. C. Bentley, 2014]. *Formatting Monthly Magazine, 17*(1), 32-34. doi: 10.1234567890

A Quick Overview : **Reviews of Films**

General Template

Last name of reviewer, First Initial. Middle Initial. (year). Title of review [Review of the television broadcast *Title of film,* produced by Author First Initial. Author Middle Initial. Author Last Name, Year of Release]. *Title of work, Volume Number,* page numbers.

Example:

Anders, J. C. (2014). Writing perfect papers. [Review of the film *The hardest paper ever written,* produced by B. C. Bentley, 2014]. *Formatting Monthly Magazine, 17,* 32-34.

In text citations for Reviews follows the same format as the in text citations as books. For in text citation formatting:

- For Reviews with one author, see page 55
- For Reviews with two authors, see page 65
- For Reviews with three authors, see page 76

Reviews of Film

Review of a Film, One Author

Anders, J. C. (2014). Writing perfect papers. [Review of the film *The hardest paper ever written,* produced by B. C. Bentley, 2014]. *Formatting Monthly Magazine, 17,* 32-34.

Review of a Film, One Author, with Index Number

Anders, J. C. (2014). Writing perfect papers. [Review of the film *The hardest paper ever written,* produced by B. C. Bentley, 2014]. *Formatting Monthly Magazine, 17*(1), 32-34.

Review of a Film, no Date

Anders, J. C. (n.d.). Writing perfect papers. [Review of the film *The hardest paper ever written,* produced by B. C. Bentley, 2014]. *Formatting Monthly Magazine, 17,* 32-34.

Review of a Film, No Author, with Index Number

[Review of the film *The hardest paper ever written,* produced by B. C. Bentley, 2014]. (2014). Writing perfect papers. *Formatting Monthly Magazine, 17*(1), 32-34.

Online Review of a Film

Anders, J. C. (2014). Writing perfect papers. [Review of the film *The hardest paper ever written,* produced by B. C. Bentley, 2014]. *Formatting Monthly Magazine,17,* 32-34. Retrieved from www.youversustheworld.com

Online Review of a Film with DOI

Anders, J. C. (2014). Writing perfect papers. [Review of the film *The hardest paper ever written,* produced by B. C. Bentley, 2014]. *Formatting Monthly Magazine, 17,* 32-34. doi: 10.1234567890

Online Review of a Film, No Title, with Index Number, with DOI

Anders, J. C. (2014). [Review of the film *The hardest paper ever written,* produced by B. C. Bentley, 2014]. *Formatting Monthly Magazine, 17*(1), 32-34. doi: 10.1234567890

A Quick Overview : **Reviews of Video Games**

General Template

Last name of reviewer, First Initial. Middle Initial. (year). Title of review [Review of the video game *Title of video game,* produced by Production Company Name, Year of Release]. *Title of work, Volume Number,* page numbers.

Example:

Anders, J. C. (2014). Why video games kill study habits. [Review of the video game *Killer papers,* produced by B. C. Bentley, 2014]. *Gamers united magazine, 17,* 32-34.

In text citations for Reviews follows the same format as the in text citations as books. For in text citation formatting:

- For Reviews with one author, see page 55
- For Reviews with two authors, see page 65
- For Reviews with three authors, see page 76

Reviews of Video Games

Review of a Video Game, One Author

Anders, J. C. (2014). Why video games kill study habits. [Review of the video game *Killer papers,* produced by B. C. Bentley, 2014]. *Gamers united magazine,17,* 32-34.

Review of a Video Game, One Author, with Index Number

Anders, J. C. (2014). Why video games kill study habits. [Review of the video game *Killer papers,* produced by B. C. Bentley, 2014]. *Gamers united magazine, 17*(1), 32-34.

Review of a Video Game, no Date

Anders, J. C. (n.d.). Why video games kill study habits. [Review of the video game *Killer papers,* produced by B. C. Bentley, 2014]. *Gamers united magazine, 17,* 32-34.

Review of a Video Game, No Author

[Review of the video game *Killer papers,* produced by B. C. Bentley, 2014]. (2014). Why video games kill study habits. *Gamers united magazine, 17,* 32-34.

Review of a Video Game, No Author, No Title, with Index Number

[Review of the video game *Killer papers,* produced by B. C. Bentley, 2014]. (2014). *Gamers united magazine, 17*(1), 32-34.

Online Review of a Video Game with DOI

Anders, J. C. (2014). Why video games kill study habits. [Review of the video game *Killer papers,* produced by B. C. Bentley, 2014]. *Gamers united magazine, 17,* 32-34. doi: 10.1234567890

Online Review of a Video Game, No Author, No Title, with DOI

[Review of the video game *Killer papers,* produced by B. C. Bentley, 2014]. (2014). doi: 10.1234567890

Online Review of a Video Game, no DOI

Anders, J. C. (2014). Why video games kill study habits. [Review of the video game *Killer papers,* produced by B. C. Bentley, 2014]. *Gamers united magazine,17,* 32-34. Retrieved from www.youversustheworld.com

Online Review of a Video Game, No Author, No Title, no DOI

[Review of the video game *Killer papers,* produced by B. C. Bentley, 2014]. (2014). Retrieved from http://www.youversustheworld.com

Online Review of a Video Game, No Title, with DOI

Anders, J. C. (2014). [Review of the video game *Killer papers,* produced by B. C. Bentley, 2014]. *Gamers united magazine, 17*(1), 32-34. doi:10.1234567890

A Quick Overview : **Peer Commentary**

General Template

Last name of reviewer, First Initial. Middle Initial. (year). Title of review [Peer commentary on the paper "Title of article" by Author First Initial. Author Middle Initial. Author Last Name]. Retrieved from www.nameofurl.com

Example:

Anders, J. C. (2014). *The hardest paper ever written* [Peer commentary on the paper "Writing perfect papers" by B. C. Bentley]. Retrieved from http://www.youversustheworld.com

In text citations for Reviews follows the same format as the in text citations as books. For in text citation formatting:

- For Reviews with one author, see page 55
- For Reviews with two authors, see page 65
- For Reviews with three authors, see page 76

Peer Commentary on Articles

Peer Commentary on an Article, One Author

Anders, J. C. (2014). *The hardest paper ever written* [Peer commentary on the paper "Writing perfect papers" by B. C. Bentley]. Retrieved from http://www.youversustheworld.com

Peer Commentary on an Article, Two Authors

Anders, J. C. (2014). *The hardest paper ever written* [Peer commentary on the paper "Writing perfect papers" by B. C. Bentley & A. N. Whitehead]. Retrieved from http://www.youversustheworld.com

Peer Commentary on an Article, Three Authors

Anders, J. C. (2014). *The hardest paper ever written* [Peer commentary on the paper "Writing perfect papers" by B. C. Bentley, A. N. Whitehead, & R. J. Smith]. Retrieved from http://www.youversustheworld.com

Peer Commentary on an Article, no Date

Anders, J. C. (n.d.). *The hardest paper ever written* [Peer commentary on the paper "Writing perfect papers" by B. C. Bentley]. Retrieved from http://www.youversustheworld.com

Peer Commentary on an Article with DOI

Anders, J. C. (2014). *The hardest paper ever written* [Peer commentary on the paper "Writing perfect papers" by B. C. Bentley]. doi:10.1234567890

Chapter 4 - Media References

References for Media

A Quick Overview : ***Motion Pictures***

General Template

Primary Contributor Last Name, First Initial. Middle Initial. (Role). (Year). *Title of motion picture* [Medium]. Country of Origin: Studio

Example:

Anders, J. C. (Director). (2014). *Where the wild formats are* [DVD]. Canada: APA Studios.

In text citations for Motion Pictures follows the same format as the in text citations as books. For in text citation formatting:

- For Motion Pictures with one Directors/Producers, see page 55
- For Motion Pictures with two Directors/Producers, see page 65
- For Motion Pictures with three Directors/Producers, see page 76

References for Motion Pictures

Motion Picture

Anders, J. C. (Director). (2014). *Where the wild formats are* [DVD]. Canada: APA Studios.

Motion Picture with Director and Producer

Wilhelm, R. D. (Producer), & Anders, J. C. (Director). (2014). *Where the wild formats are* [DVD]. Canada: APA Studios.

Motion Picture with Two Producers and Director

Wilhelm, R. D., Selhime, D. R. (Producers), & Anders, J. C. (Director). (2014). *Where the wild formats are* [DVD]. Canada: APA Studios.

Motion Picture Found Online

Anders, J. C. (Director). (2014). *Where the wild formats are* [DVD]. Available from http://www.netflix.com

A Quick Overview : ***Music Recordings***

General Template

Writer Last Name, First Initial. Middle Initial. (Copyright Year). Title of song [Recorded by First Initial. Middle Initial. Last Name of Artist if different from writer]. On *Title of album* [Medium] Location: Label. (Date of recording if different from song copyright)

Example:

Music Recording

Anders, J. C. (2014). I format like a tiger [Recorded by G. C. Hipster]. On *Terrible titles* [CD]. Denver, CO: APA Records.

In Text Citation Example:

"Terrible Titles" (Anders, 2014, Track 8)

References for Music Recordings

Music Recording

Anders, J. C. (2014). I format like a tiger [Recorded by G. C. Hipster]. On *Terrible titles* [CD]. Denver, CO: APA Records.

In Text Citation:

"Terrible Titles" (Anders, 2014, Track 8)

Music Recording, no Date

Anders, J. C. (n.d.). I format like a tiger [Recorded by G. C. Hipster]. On *Terrible titles* [CD]. Denver, CO: APA Records.

Music Recording, Record Format

Anders, J. C. (2014). I format like a tiger [Recorded by G. C. Hipster]. On *Terrible titles* [Record]. Denver, CO: APA Records.

Music Recording, MP3 Format

Anders, J. C. (2014). I format like a tiger [Recorded by G. C. Hipster]. On *Terrible titles* [MP3 file]. Denver, CO: APA Records.

Music Recording from Online Source

Anders, J. C. (2014). I format like a tiger [Recorded by G. C. Hipster]. On *Terrible titles* [CD]. Retrieved from www.itunes.com

Music Recording, Writer and Artist are the Same

Anders, J. C. (2014). I format like a tiger. On *Terrible titles* [Cassette]. Denver, CO: APA Records.

Music Recording, Dual Writing Credits

Anders, J. C. & Pop, Z. Z. (2014). I format like a tiger [Recorded by G. C. Hipster]. On *Terrible titles* [CD]. Denver, CO: APA Records.

Music Recording, Date of Recording Different Than Copyright Year

Anders, J. C. (2014). I format like a tiger [Recorded by G. C. Hipster]. On *Terrible titles* [CD]. Denver, CO: APA Records. (2012)

Music Recording, Single Track on Album

Anders, J. C. (2014). I format like a tiger [Recorded by G. C. Hipster]. On *Terrible titles* [CD]. Denver, CO: APA Records.

Music Recording, Single Track on Album, Online Source

Anders, J. C. (2014). I format like a tiger [Recorded by G. C. Hipster]. On *Terrible titles* [CD]. Retrieved from http://www.itunes.com

Music Recording, Full Album

Anders, J. C. (2014). *Terrible titles* [Recorded by G. C. Hipster; CD]. Denver, CO: APA Records.

Music Recording, Full Album, Online Source

Anders, J. C. (2014). *Terrible titles* [Recorded by G. C. Hipster; Record]. Retrieved from http://www.amazon.com

A Quick Overview : **Podcasts**

General Template

Producer Last Name, First Initial. Middle Initial. (Year, Month Day). *Crazy podcasts on formatting* [Audio podcast]. Retrieved from http://www.iTunes.com/

Example:

Anders, J. C. (Producer). (2014, January 10). *Crazy podcast on formatting* [Audio podcast]. Retrieved from http://www.iTunes.com/podcast

In text citations for Podcasts follows the same format as the in text citations as books. For in text citation formatting:

- For Podcasts with one Directors/Producers, see page 55
- For Podcasts with two Directors/Producers, see page 65
- For Podcasts with three Directors/Producers, see page 76

References for Podcasts

Podcast

Anders, J. C. (Producer). (2014, January 10). *Crazy podcast on formatting* [Audio podcast]. Retrieved from http://www.iTunes.com/podcast

Podcast, no Date

Anders, J. C. (Producer). (n.d.). *Crazy podcast on formatting* [Audio podcast]. Retrieved from http://www.iTunes.com/

Podcast, with Producer and Writer

Anders, J. C. (Producer), & White, M. T. (Writer). (2014, January 10). *Crazy podcast on formatting* [Audio podcast]. Retrieved from http://www.iTunes.com/postcastwithproducerandwriter

Podcast, no Producer

Crazy podcast on formatting [Audio podcast]. (2014, January 10). Retrieved from http://www.iTunes.com/podcastwithnoproducer

Podcast, with Organization as Producer

Siristar. (Producer). (2014, January 10). *While we gently format* [Audio podcast]. Retrieved from http://www.iTunes.com/

Video Podcast

Anders, J. C. (2014, January 10). *Crazy podcast on formatting* [Video podcast]. Retrieved from http://www.iTunes.com/

Video Podcast, no Individual Writer or Producer

Crazy podcast on formatting [Video podcast]. Retrieved from http://www.iTunes.com

A Quick Overview : ***Television Series***

General Template

Last Name of Writer, First Initial. Middle Initial. (Writer), & Last name, First Initial. Middle Initial (Director). (Year) Name of episode [Television series episode]. In First Initial. Last Name of Producer (Executive producer), *Name of television series.* City, State Abbreviation of production: Broadcast Company.

Example:

Anders, J. C. (Producer). (2014). Holy formatting in a digital age [Television broadcast]. Chicago, IL: CBS Broadcasting.

In text citations for Televison Broadcasts follows the same format as the in text citations as books. For in text citation formatting:

- For Television Broadcasts with one Directors/Producers, see page 55
- For Television Broadcasts with two Directors/Producers, see page 65
- For Television Broadcasts with three Directors/Producers, see page 76

Television Series

Television Series, Entire Episode

Anders, J. C. (Producer). (2014). Holy formatting in a digital age [Television broadcast]. Chicago, IL: CBS Broadcasting.

Television Broadcast

Anders, J. C. (Producer). (2014, December 8). *The news show* [Television broadcast]. Chicago, IL.: CBS Broadcasting

Episode from Television Series

Anders, J. C. (Writer). (2014). Holy formatting in a digital age [Television series episode]. In R. T. Smith (Producer), *Taking formatting way too seriously*. Chicago, IL: CBS Broadcasting.

Webisode from Television Series

Anders, J. C. (Writer). (2014). Holy formatting in a digital age [Television series webisode]. In R. T. Smith (Producer), *Taking formatting way too seriously*. Chicago, IL: CBS Broadcasting.

Episode from Television Series, with Director

Anders, J. C. (Writer), & France, R. T. (Director). (2014). Holy formatting in a digital age [Television series episode]. In R. T. Smith (Producer), *Taking formatting way too seriously*. Chicago, IL: CBS Broadcasting.

Episode from Television Series, with Two Writers

Anders, J. C. (Writer), Rolanz, Q. M. (Writer),. (2014). Holy formatting in a digital age [Television series episode]. In R. T. Smith (Producer), *Taking formatting way too seriously*. Chicago, IL: CBS Broadcasting.

Maps

General format

Name of Organization that Produced the Map (Cartographer). (Year). Name of map [Type of map]. Retrieved from http://www.youversustheworld.com/maps.pdf

Weld County Oil and Gas Geological Survey Team (Cartographer). (2014). Oil and gas locations in Weld County [GIS map]. Retrieved from http://www.co.weldcounty.com

Demographic Map

Weld County Oil and Gas Geological Survey Team (Cartographer). (2014). Oil and gas locations in Weld County [Demographic map]. Retrieved from http://www.co.weldcounty.com

Other Media

Speech Recording or Audio File

Matkovich, S. R. (2014, May 6). *A course in formatting* [Audio file]. Retrieved from http://www.youversustheworld.com

Interview Recording - Original Recording on Cassette, Found Online

Anders, J. A. (2014, May 6). *Interview with Richard Beiler* (S. Matkovich, Interviewer) [Cassette]. Retrieved from http://www.youversustheworld.com

PowerPoint Presentation

Anders, J. (2014). *Getting writing right* [PowerPoint slides]. Retrieved from http://www.youversustheworld.com

Painting

Anders, J. C. (2014). *Starry Skies* [Painting]. Retrieved from http://www.youversustheworld.com

Photograph

Kraus, A. (2014). *Fireworks by night* [Photograph]. Retrieved from http://www.youversustheworld.com

Mobilc App for Phonc, Tablct, Etc.

Anders, J. (2014). Format App for iPhone (Version 1.0) [Mobile application software]. Retrieved from http://www.itunes.com/formatapp

Mobile App for Phone, Tablet, Etc. From Corporation

Inventiveapp. (2014). Format App for iPhone (Version 1.0) [Mobile application software]. Retrieved from http://www.itunes.com/formatapp

In Text Citation Example

("Inventiveapp," 2014)

Video Webcast

Anders, J. C. (2014). *Where the wild formats are* [Video webcast]. Canada: APA Studios.

Computer Software

APA Formatting Software (Version 1.4) [Computer software]. Buffalo Grove, IL: Anchor Software.

Chapter 5 - References for Unpublished Manuscripts

References for Unpublished Works

A Quick Overview : **Unpublished Works**

General Template

Last Name of Author, First Initial. Middle Initial. (Year). *Title of work.* Unpublished manuscript.

Example:

Anders, J. C. (2014). *Formatting for smart people.* Unpublished manuscript.

In text citations for Unpublished Works follows the same format as the in text citations as books. For in text citation formatting:

- For Unpublished Works without an author, see page 13
- For Unpublished Works with one author, see page 55
- For Unpublished Works with two authors, see page 65
- For Unpublished Works with three authors, see page 76

Unpublished Works

Unpublished Manuscript, No Author

Formatting for smart people. (2014). Unpublished manuscript.

Unpublished Manuscript, No Author, No Date

Formatting for smart people. (n.d.). Unpublished manuscript.

Unpublished Manuscript, No Author, University Cited

Formatting for smart people. (2014). Unpublished manuscript, Department of Anatomy and Physiology, University of Montana, Billings, MT.

Manuscript Submitted for Publication, No Author

Formatting for smart people. (2014). Manuscript submitted for publication.

Manuscript Being Prepared for Publication, No Author

Formatting for smart people. (2014). Manuscript being prepared for publication.

Unpublished Manuscripts with One Author

Unpublished Manuscript, One Author

Anders, J. C. (2014). *Formatting for smart people.* Unpublished manuscript.

Unpublished Manuscript, One Author, No Date

Anders, J. C. (n.d.). *Formatting for smart people.* Unpublished manuscript.

Unpublished Manuscript, One Author, University Cited

Anders, J. C. (2014). *Formatting for smart people.* Unpublished manuscript, Department of Anatomy and Physiology, University of Montana, Billings, MT, US.

Unpublished Raw Data from Study, One Author

Anders, J. C. (2014). *Formatting for ordinary people.* Unpublished raw data.

Unpublished Raw Data from Study, One Author, No Title

Anders, J. C. (2014). [Description of data]. Unpublished raw data.

Unpublished Papers or Lectures from an Archive or Personal Collection, One Author

Anders, J. C. (2014). *Formatting for smart people.* Dan Willard Letters (Folder 87). Billings University Archives, University of Montana, Billings, MT.

Manuscript Submitted for Publication, One Author

Anders, J. C. (2014). *Formatting for smart people.* Manuscript submitted for publication.

Manuscript Being Prepared for Publication, One Author

Anders, J. C. (2014). *Formatting for smart people.* Manuscript being prepared for publication.

Self Archived Work, One Author

Anders, J. C. (2014). *Formatting for ordinary people.* Retrieved from http://www.youversustheworld.com

Informally Published, from ERIC, One Author

Anders, J. C., & Beiler, R. C. (2014). *Formatting for smart people.* Retrieved from ERIC Database. (ED123456)

Unpublished Manuscript, Two Authors

Unpublished Manuscript, Two Authors

Anders, J. C., & Beiler, R. C. (2014). *Formatting for smart people.* Unpublished manuscript.

Unpublished Manuscript, Two Authors, No Date

Anders, J. C., & Beiler, R. C. (n.d.). *Formatting for smart people.* Unpublished manuscript.

Unpublished Manuscript, Two Authors, University Cited

Anders, J. C., & Beiler, R. C. (2014). *Formatting for smart people.* Unpublished manuscript, Department of Anatomy and Physiology, University of Montana, Billings, MT, US.

Unpublished Raw Data from Study, Two Authors

Anders, J. C., & Beiler, R. C. (2014). *Formatting for ordinary people.* Unpublished raw data.

Unpublished Raw Data from Study, Two Authors, No Title

Anders, J. C., & Beiler, R. C. (2014). [Description of data]. Unpublished raw data.

Unpublished Papers or Lectures from an Archive or Personal Collection, Two Authors

Anders, J. C., & Beiler, R. C. (2014). *Formatting for smart people.* Dan Willard Letters (Folder 87). Billings University Archives, University of Montana, Billings, MT.

Manuscript Submitted for Publication, Two Authors

Anders, J. C., & Beiler, R. C. (2014). *Formatting for smart people.* Manuscript submitted for publication.

Manuscript Being Prepared for Publication, Two Authors

Anders, J. C., & Beiler, R. C. (2014). *Formatting for smart people.* Manuscript being prepared for publication.

Self Archived Work, Two Authors

Anders, J. C., & Beiler, R. C. (2014). *Formatting for ordinary people.* Retrieved from http://www.youversustheworld.com

Informally Published, from ERIC, Two Authors

Anders, J. C., & Beiler, R. C. (2014). *Formatting for smart people.* Retrieved from ERIC Database. (ED123456)

Unpublished Manuscript, Three Authors

Unpublished Manuscript, Three Authors

Anders, J. C., Johnson, A. A., & Beiler, R. C. (2014). *Formatting for smart people.* Unpublished manuscript.

Unpublished Manuscript, Three Authors, No Date

Anders, J. C., Johnson, A. A., & Beiler, R. C. (n.d.). *Formatting for smart people.* Unpublished manuscript.

Unpublished Manuscript, Three Authors, University Cited

Anders, J. C., Johnson, A. A., & Beiler, R. C. (2014). *Formatting for ordinary people.* Unpublished manuscript, Department of Anatomy and Physiology, University of Montana, Billings, MT, US.

Unpublished Raw Data from Study, Three Authors

Anders, J. C., Johnson, A. A., & Beiler, R. C. (2014). *Formatting for ordinary people.* Unpublished raw data.

Unpublished Raw Data from Study, Three Authors, No Title

Anders, J. C., Johnson, A. A., & Beiler, R. C. (2014). [Description of data]. Unpublished raw data.

Unpublished Papers or Lectures from an Archive or Personal Collection, Three Authors

Anders, J. C., Johnson, A. A., & Beiler, R. C. (2014). *Formatting for smart people.* Dan Willard Letters (Box 12, Folder 87). Billings University Archives, University of Montana, Billings, MT.

Manuscript Submitted for Publication, Three Authors

Anders, J. C., Johnson, A. A., & Beiler, R. C. (2014). *Formatting for smart people.* Manuscript submitted for publication.

Manuscript Being Prepared for Publication, Three Authors

Anders, J. C., Johnson, A. A., & Beiler, R. C. (2014). *Formatting for smart people.* Manuscript being prepared for publication.

Self Archived Work, Three Authors

Anders, J. C., Johnson, A. A., & Beiler, R. C. (2014). *Formatting for ordinary people.* Retrieved from http://www.youversustheworld.com

Informally Published, from ERIC, Three Authors

Anders, J. C., Johnson, A. A., & Beiler, R. C. (2014). *Formatting for smart people.* Retrieved from ERIC Database. (ED123456)

Chapter 6 - References for Web Pages, Online Posts & Collections and Archived Works

A Quick Overview : ***Online Posts & Web Pages***

General Template

Authors Last Name, First Initial. Middle Initial. (Year, Month Day). Title of post [Description of form]. Retrieved from http://www.addressofwebsite.com

Example:

Anders, J. C. (2014, May 6). Why metaphysics belongs in the university [Online forum comment]. Retrieved from http://www.youversustheworld.com

In text citations for Online Posts follows the same format as the in text citations as books. For in text citation formatting:

- For Online Posts without an author, see page 13
- For Online Posts with one author, see page 55
- For Online Posts with two authors, see page 65
- For Online Posts with three authors, see page 76

Web Page: General Template

Website with Author

Author Last Name, First Initials. (Year of Publication). *Title of website.* Retrieved from URL

Anders, J. (2012). APA rules. Retrieved from http://www.denverpost.com

Website without Author

Title of website. (Year of Publication). Retrieved from URL

In text citations for web pages with or without an author:

Example #1 (with an author; paraphrase)

According to Anders (2012), writing in APA format is an easy way to organize a research paper.

Example #2 (with an author; direct quote)

Anders (2012) stated, "Writing in APA format is an easy way to organize a research paper" (APA Rules, para. 3).

Example #3 (no author)

Note: if no author is available, the APA asks that we use the name of the organization, corporation, agency, etc.

Writing in APA is really easy when we have the tools that we need (National Writers Association, 2012).

Example #4: (no author, direct quote)

The National Writers Association (2012) notes, "Writing in APA format is easy when we have all the tools we need" (Research Writing: APA, para. 4).

Message Boards

Message Posted to a Newsgroup

Anders, J. C. (2014, May 6). Why metaphysics belongs in the university [Newsgroup comment]. Retrieved from http://www.youversustheworld.com

Message Posted to an Online Forum

Anders, J. C. (2014, May 6). Why metaphysics belongs in the university [Online forum comment]. Retrieved from http://www.youversustheworld.com

Message Posted to a Discussion Group

Anders, J. C. (2014, May 6). Why metaphysics belongs in the university [Discussion group comment]. Retrieved from http://www.youversustheworld.com

Message Posted to an E-mail List

Anders, J. C. (2014, May 6). Why metaphysics belongs in the university [Electronic mailing list message]. Retrieved from http://www.youversustheworld.com

Web Pages and Blog Posts

General Template

Anders, J. C. (2014, May 6). Why metaphysics belongs in the university [Blog post]. Retrieved from http://www.youversustheworld.com

Basic Web Page with Known Author

Anders, J. (2012). APA rules. Retrieved from http://www.denverpost.com

Basic Web Page with No Author

APA rules. (2011). Retrieved from http://www.aparules.com

Blog Post, No Author, No Title

[Metaphysics in the university]. (2014). Retrieved from http://www.youversustheworld.com

Blog Post, no Date

Anders, J. C. (n.d.). Why metaphysics belongs in the university [Blog post]. Retrieved from http://www.youversustheworld.com

Blog Post, no Date, Good Estimate Can Be Made

Anders, J. C. (ca. 2014). Why metaphysics belongs in the university [Blog post]. Retrieved from http://www.youversustheworld.com

Comment Posted to a Blog

Screenname. (2014, May 6). Why metaphysics belongs in the university [Blog comment]. Retrieved from http://www.youversustheworld.com

Blog Post with Organization as Author

MarketCorp. (2014, May 6). Why metaphysics belongs in the university. [Blog post]. Retrieved from http://www.youversustheworld.com

Blog Post, Missing Title

Anders, J. C. (2014, May 6). [Metaphysics in the university]. Retrieved from http://www.youversustheworld.com

Blog Post, No Author, No Title

[Metaphysics in the university]. (2014). Retrieved from http://www.youversustheworld.com

Video Blog or Vlog Post

Anders, J. C. (2014, May 6). Why metaphysics belongs in the university [Video file]. Retrieved from http://www.youversustheworld.com

Video Post, no Date

Anders, J. C. (n.d.). Why metaphysics belongs in the university [Video file]. Retrieved from http://www.youversustheworld.com

Comment Posted to a Video File

Anders, J. C. (2014, May 6). Why metaphysics belongs in the university [Online forum comment]. Retrieved from http://www.youversustheworld.com

Video Post with Organization as Author

MarketCorp. (2014, May 6). Why metaphysics belongs in the university. [Video file]. Retrieved from http://www.youversustheworld.com

Video Post, Missing Title

Anders, J. C. (2014, May 6). [Metaphysics in the university]. Retrieved from http://www.youversustheworld.com

Video Post, no Date, Good Estimate Can Be Made

Anders, J. C. (ca. 2014). Why metaphysics belongs in the university [Video file]. Retrieved from http://www.youversustheworld.com

Video Blog with 2 Presenters

Anders, J. C., & Kidd, B. B. (2014, May 6). Why metaphysics belongs in the university [Video file]. Retrieved from http://youversustheworld.com

A Quick Overview : ***Collections and Archived Works***

General Template

Author Last Name, First Initial. Middle Initial. (Year, Month Day). *Title of collection* [Description of material]. Name of Collection (Call number, Box number, File name, other archival information). Name of Repository, Location.

Example:

Anders, J. C. (2014, May 6). [Letter to Rolf Anderson]. Billings University Archive (Box 45, Folder 19), Billings, MT.

In text citations for Collections and Archived Works follow the same format as the in text citations as books. For in text citation formatting:

- For Collections and Archived Works without an author, see page 13
- For Collections and Archived Works with one author, see page 55
- For Collections and Archived Works with two authors, see page 65
- For Collections and Archived Works with three authors, see page 76

Collections and Archived Works

Letter from Repository

Anders, J. C. (2014, May 6). [Letter to Rolf Anderson]. Billings University Archive (Box 45, Folder 19), Billings, MT.

Letter from Private Collection

Anders, J. C. (2014, May 6). [Letter to Rolf Anderson (D. Willard, Trans.)]. Copy in possession of Dan Willard Estate.

Collection of Letters from an Archive

Anders, J. C. (2012-2014). Correspondence. Rolf Anderson Letters (HUG 1234.56). Billings University Archives, Billings, MT.

Archived Work

Anders, J. C. (2014, May 6). *Working for a living* [Letter]. Rolf Anderson Collection (R5160, Box 77). Billings University Archives, Billings, MT.

Archived Work, No Author

Working for a living [Letter]. (2014, May 6). Rolf Anderson Collection (R5160, Box 7). Billings University Library, Billings, MT.

Archived Work, No Author, No Date

Working for a living [Letter]. (n.d.). Rolf Anderson Collection (R5160, Box 7). Billings University Library, Billings, MT.

Archived Work with Reasonably Certain Author and Date, Though Not Stated

[Anders, J. C.?]. [ca. 2014]. *Working for a living.* Rolf Anderson Collection. Billings University Archives, Billings, MT.

Archived Work with Corporate Author

Agreeing to disagree as a group. (2014, May 6). *Meeting of the Agreeing Minds.* Rolf Anderson Papers (R5160). Billings University Archives, Billings, MT.

Archived Interview

Anders, J. C. (1972, May 6). Interview by R. Anderson [Tape recording]. Watergate Phone Records, Billings University. Billings University Archives, Billings, MT.

Archived Interview Transcript

Anders, J. C. (1972). *Agreeing to disagree.* Watergate Phone Recordings (File 987), University of Billings, Billings, MT.

Archived Newspaper Article

Working for a living. (2014, May 6). [Clipping from Billings Gazette, newspaper]. Copy in Billings University Archive.

Archived Photographs

[Photographs of Rolf Anderson]. (ca. 1998-2014). Rolf Anderson Collection (Box 4555, Folder 1899). Billings University Archives, Billings University, Billings, MT.

Chapter 7 - References for Social Media

A Quick Overview : ***Social Media***

General Template

Author Last name, First Initial. [Screen name]. (Date). Title of post: link to post [Type of post]. Retrieved from http://www.nameofwebsite.com

Example:

JAnders. (2014, May 6). Description of post content: http://shorturlifpossible.com [Tweet]. Retrieved from http://www.twitter.com

In text citations differ depending on the website and the type of post.

Generally, Twitter posts will look like this:

(Matkovich, 2011) or (Last name, Year of Post)

Facebook:

(Last name, Year of Post). If post is a company, (Ameritrade, 2011)

References for Twitter

Twitter Update/Tweet, Author's Name Known

Anders, J. [JAnders]. (2014, May 6). Description of post content: http://shorturlifpossible [Tweet]. Retrieved from http://www.twitter.com

Twitter Update/Tweet, Author's Name Known, No Date

Anders, J. [JAnders]. (n.d.). Description of post content: http://shorturlifpossible [Tweet]. Retrieved from http://www.twitter.com

Twitter Update/Tweet, Author's Name Unknown (Use Screen Name)

JAnders. (2014, May 6). Description of post content: http://shorturlifpossible.com [Tweet]. Retrieved from http://www.twitter.com

Twitter Update/Tweet, Author's Name Unknown (Use Screen Name), Date Reasonably Guessed

JAnders. (ca. 2014). Description of post content: http://shorturlifpossible.com [Tweet]. Retrieved from http://www.twitter.com

Twitter Update/Tweet, Author's Name as Company or Corporation

United Parcel Service. (2014, May 6). Description of post content: http://shorturlifpossible [Tweet]. Retrieved from http://www.twitter.com

Multiple Twitter Updates/Tweets from Same Author or Organization

JAnders. (2014a). Alphabetize by title and add letter after date http://shorturlifpossible.com [Tweet]. Retrieved from http://www.twitter.com

JAnders. (2014b). Be sure to alphabetize by title and add letter after date : http://shorturlifpossible.com [Tweet]. Retrieved from http://www.twitter.com

Facebook References

Facebook Status Update, Author's Name Known

Anders, J. [John]. (2014, May 6). Write out status update here [Facebook status update]. Retrieved from https://www.facebook.com/APAMadeEasy?ref=hl

Facebook Page, Author's Name Known

Anders, J. [John]. (2014, May 6). Write out status update here [Facebook page]. Retrieved from https://www.facebook.com/APAMadeEasy?ref=hl

Facebook Note, Author's Name Known

Anders, J. [John]. (2014, May 6). Write out status update here [Facebook note]. Retrieved from https://www.facebook.com/APAMadeEasy?ref=hl

Facebook Status Update, Author's Name Known, No Date

Anders, J. [John]. (n.d.). Write out status update here [Facebook status update]. Retrieved from https://www.facebook.com/APAMadeEasy?ref=hl

Facebook Status Update, Author's Name Unknown (Use Screen Name)

JAnders. (2014, May 6). Write out status update here [Facebook status update]. Retrieved from https://www.facebook.com/APAMadeEasy?ref=hl

Facebook Status Update, Author as Company or Corporation

APA Made Easy. (2014, May 6). Write out status update here [Facebook status update]. Retrieved from https://www.facebook.com/APAMadeEasy?ref=hl

Facebook Status Update, Author as Company or Corporation, Date Reasonably Guessed

APA Made Easy. (ca. 2014). Write out status update here [Facebook status update]. Retrieved from https://www.facebook.com/APAMadeEasy?ref=hl

Multiple Facebook Status Updates from Same Author or Organization

JAnders. (2014a). Alphabetize by title and add letter after date : http://shorturlifpossible.com [Facebook status update]. Retrieved from http://www.facebook.com.com/apamadeeasy

JAnders. (2014b). Be sure to alphabetize by title and add letter after date : http://shorturlifpossible.com [Facebook status update]. Retrieved from http://www.facebook.com/apamadeeasy

In text citations for more than one post:

(JAnders, 2014a)

(JAnders, 2014b)

Comment on Facebook Status Update - See Personal Communication Section

Facebook Application

Farmersville. (2014). Fake farming [Facebook application]. Retrieved from http://apps.facebook.com/fakefarming

Chapter 8 - References for Legal Documents

A Quick Overview : ***Legal References***

General Template

Name v. Name, Volume Source Page (Court Date).

Example:

Anders v. Beiler, 766 F. Supp. 998 (E.D. Ill. 1988).

In Text Citation Example - Documents

For court cases, an in text citation includes the name of the case and year or years in which the case was settled:

(*Anders v. Beiler*, 1998/2014).

Alternatively,
Anders v. Beiler (1998/2014) states …

In Text Citation Examples:

For statutes, provide the name of the act with the year of the act. For example,

Right to Privacy Act (1976)

Alternatively:
The Right to Privacy Act of 1976

References for Legal Documents:

In Text Citation Examples:

For court cases, an in text citation includes the name of the case and year or years in which the case was settled:

(*Anders v. Beiler*, 1998/2014).

Alternatively,

Anders v. Beiler (1998/2014) states …

Bluebook Rule 10

Court Decisions

Anders v. Beiler, 766 F. Supp. 998 (E.D. Ill. 1988).

Appealed Case

Anders v. Beiler, 618 F. Supp. 998 (D. Ca. 2004), *aff'd*, 812 F.3d 900 (9th Cir. 2014).

Unreported Decision

Anders v. Beiler, No. 88-1001 (3d Cir. Feb. 8, 1999).

Unreported Decision with Record Number

Anders v. Beiler, No. 88-1001, 1999 U.S. Dist. LEXIS 12345, at *3 (E.D. Co. June 22, 1997).

Unreported Decision with no Record Number

Anders v. Beiler, No. 88-1001, (D. Ca. Feb. 31, 1995) (LEXIS, Billings library, Dist file).

State Trial Court Opinion

Anders v. Beiler, 6 Ill. D. & C.5th 199 (C.P. Billings County 2014).

Federal District Court Opinion

Anders v. Beiler, 777 F. Supp. 987 (S.D. Ca. 2014).

Case Appealed to the State Supreme Court

Anders v. Beiler, 895 Ca. 211, 288 S.E.3d 121 (2011).

Case Appealed to the State Court of Appeals

Anders v. Beiler, 895 S.E.3d 122 (Ca. Ct. App. 2011).

Cases Decided by the U.S. Supreme Court

Anders v. Beiler, 894 U.S. 459 (1987).

Statutes

Bluebook Rule 12

Reference of a Statute

Right to Privacy Act, 55 U.S.C. § 4044 (1976).

Reference of a Statute in a State Code

Right to Privacy Act, 5 Ca. Stat. Ann. §§ 77-1001-1234 (1945 & Supp. 2001).

Reference to a Statute in a Federal Code

Right to Privacy Act, 67 U.S.C.A. § 12345 *et seq.* (West 2007).

Session Law Citation

Right to Privacy Act, Pub. L. No. 202-299, § 6, 44 Stat. 971 (2000).

Patents

Anders, J. C. (2014). U. S. Patent No. 445,978. Washington DC: U.S. Patent and Trademark Office.

In text example for a patent would look like this:

U.S. Patent No. 445,978 (2014)

-Or-

(U.S. Patent No. 445,978, 2014)

Chapter 9 - Technical and Research Reports

A Quick Overview : ***Technical and Research Reports***

General Template

Author Last Name, First Initial. (Year). *Title of work* (Report No. xyz). City, State Initials: Publisher Name.

Example:

Food and Drug Administration. (2014). *Effects of bovine growth hormone on food supply* (FDA Publication No. 01-345). Washington DC: Government Printing Office.

In text citations for Technical/Research Reports follow the same format as the in text citations as books. For in text citation formatting:

- For Technical/Research Reports without an author, see page 13
- For Technical/Research Reports with one author, see page 55
- For Technical/Research Reports with two authors, see page 65
- For Technical/Research Reports with three authors, see page 76

Technical and Research Reports

General Authored Report

Anders, J. (2014). *Formatting reports in APA* (Report No. 123.4). Billings, MT: Anchor Press.

Report from Corporate Author

Corporation for Public Broadcasting. (2014). *Report on formatting in a corporate setting* (Report No. 123.4). Billings, MT: Anchor Press.

Corporate Author, Government Report

Food and Drug Administration. (2014). *Effects of bovine growth hormone on food supply* (FDA Publication No. 01-345). Washington DC: Government Printing Office.

Report from Institutional Archive

Anders, J. (2014). *The effect of meteors on Earth's atmosphere* (NASA Report 4.187). Retrieved from University of Billings, Billings University Library: http://www.billingslibrary.nasastudy.org/library/meteor.pdf

Issue Brief

Center for Immigrant Integration. (2014, May). *Availablility of part time employment for non-resident citizens* (Issue Brief No. 378). Billings, MT: Billings University Press.

Authored Report from Nongovernmental Organziation

Anders, J. (2014). *Finding interesting formatting structures* (Research Report No. 6.13). Retrieved from Research on Formatting Structures website: http://www.formattingandresearch.edu.ok/documents/publications

Corporate Author, Task Force

Corporation for Public Broadcasting, Task Force on Television Viewership. (2014). *Report of the Public Broadcasting Task Force of Television Viewership.* Retrieved from http://www.PBS.org/televisionviewership

Chapter 10 - Meetings and Symposia

A Quick Overview : ***Meetings and Symposia***

General Template

Contributor Last Name, First Initial. (Year, Month). Title of contribution. In First Initial. Last Name of Chairperson (Chair), *Title of symposum.* Symposium conducted at the meeting of Organization Name, Location.

Example:

Anders, J. (2014, May). *Formatting blunders.* Paper presented at Billings University Writer's Conference, Billings, MT. Abstract retreived from http://www.billingsconferencecenter.edu/papers/conference

In text citations for Meetings and Symposia follow the same format as the in text citations as Journals. For in text citation formatting:

- For Meetings and Symposia without an author, see page 147
- For Meetings and Symposia with one author, see page 154
- For Meetings and Symposia with two authors, see page 161
- For Meetings and Symposia with three authors, see page 168

Meetings and Symposia

General Format for a Symposium

Anders, J. (2014, May). Running numbers by the book. In R. Beiler (Chair), *Symposium for accounting nightmares.* Symposium conducted at the meeting of Ridgeview Classical University, Fort Collins, CO.

Paper Presentation

Matkovich, S. (2014, May). *Five mistakes smart people make.* Paper presented at the meeting of International Philosophers, Billings, MT.

Symposium Contribution

Anders, J. (2014, May). Writing and formatting. In S. Lorenzen (Chair), *Formatting intelligence.* Symposium conducted at the meeting of Christian Writers, Salem, OR.

Conference Paper Abstract, Online

Anders, J. (2014, May). *Formatting blunders.* Paper presented at Billings University Writer's Conference, Billings, MT. Abstract retreived from http:// www.billingsconferencecenter.edu/papers/conference

Proceedings Published Regularly, Online

Anders, J. (2014). The monthly review. *Proceedings of the Salem Library,* USA, 110, 12345-67890. doi:10.1234567890

Proceedings Published in Book

Anders, J. (2014). The monthly review. In R. Beiler (Ed.), *Numbers by the book: Vol. 1234. Conference for Reviewing Number at University Libraries* (pp. 10-19). doi:10.1234567890

Chapter 11

Master's Theses and Doctoral Dissertations

&

Data Sets, Software, Measurement Instruments, and Apparatus

A Quick Overview : ***Theses and Dissertations***

General Template

Contributor Last Name, First Initial. (Year). *Name of dissertation* (Doctoral dissertation). University Name, City, State Initials.

Example:

Anders, J. (2014). *Formatting for success* (Doctoral dissertation). Retrieved from ProTemp Database. (Accession No. 12345)

In text citations for Theses and Dissertations follow the same format as the in text citations as Journals. For in text citation formatting:

- For Thesis and Dissertations without an author, see page 147
- For Thesis and Dissertations with one author, see page 154
- For Thesis and Dissertations with two authors, see page 161
- For Thesis and Dissertations with three authors, see page 168

Theses and Dissertations

General Reference for Doctoral Dissertations

Anders, J. (2014). *Formatting for success* (Doctoral dissertation). Retrieved from ProTemp Database. (Accession No. 12345)

General Reference for Master's Thesis

Anders, J. (2014). *Formatting for success* (Master's thesis). Retrieved from ProTemp Database. (Accession No. 12345)

General Reference for Unpublished Doctoral Dissertations

Anders, J. (2014). *Formatting for success* (Unpublished doctoral dissertation). Montana State University, Billings, MT.

General Reference for Unpublished Master's Thesis

Anders, J. (2014). *Formatting for success* (Unpublished master's thesis). Montana State University, Billings, MT.

Master's Thesis from Commercial Database

Anders, J. (2014). *Formatting for success* (Master's thesis). Available from ProText Database. (UMI No. 123456).

Doctoral Dissertation from Institution Database

Anders, J. (2014). *Formatting for success* (Doctoral dissertation). Retrieved from http://www.universityofbillings.edu/dissertation

Doctoral Dissertation from a Website

Anders, J. (2014). *Formatting for fun* (Doctoral dissertation, Billings University). Retrieved from http://www.universityofbillings.edu/dissertation

Doctoral Thesis from a University Outside the United States

Anders, J. (2014). *Formatting for fun* (Doctoral thesis, University of Aberdeen, Aberdeen, Scotland). Retrieved from http://www.unversityofaberdeen.edu/it/thesis

Data Sets, Software, and Measurment Instruments

Apparatus

Examumin [Apparatus]. (2014). Billings, MT: Medimax.

Software

Readquik (Version 1.4) [Computer software]. Billings, MT: Quikstart Inc.

Measurement Instrument

Anders, J. (2014). METRX: Dynamic software [software]. La Mirada, CA: Metrx Systems.

Data Set

Center for Disease Control. (2014). *Effect of flue vaccine on youth population* [Data file]. Retrieved from http://www.cdc.gov/flu/population/young

Chapter 12 - Other References, Notes, and Closing Thoughts

Brochure, Online

City of Dacono. (2014). *A guide to the city of extreme sports* [Brochure]. Retrieved from http://www.youversustheworld.com

Lecture Notes, Online

Anders, J. (2014). *Getting writing right* [Lecture notes]. Retrieved from http://www.youversustheworld.com

Press Release, Online

City of Dacono. (2014, May 6). *Extreme sports in Dacono* [Press release]. Retrieved from http://www.youversustheworld.com

Supplemental Material Found Online for a Journal Article

Anders, J. A. (2014). Finding other APA sources online [Supplemental material]. *Journal of writing and formatting, 144,* 199-203. doi:10.1234567890.supp

Podcast Transcript, Online

Anders, J. (2014). *Zen and the art of formatting podcast transcript, May 6, 2014.* http:www.itunes.com/zenandtheartofformatting

Computer Software

Anders, J. (2011). Linware bible software [computer software]. Barrington, IL: Tillson.

How to work with Personal Communication

Content that cannot be recovered by another individual is often considered personal communication. Personal communication may be things like emails, phone calls, personal interviews, lectures, skype calls, etc. For your personal communication here are the two different kinds of citations:

Example #1:

P. M. Novak (personal communication, February 21, 2013) Insert the quote or paraphrased material.

Example #2:
Quote/paraphrase material (P. M. Novak, personal communication, February 21, 2013).

Another example may include using class notes, for example. If you have obtained the name of the presenter or professor, use their first initial and last name as part of your reference with "personal communication" and date of the presentation:

J. Anders, personal communication, August 3, 2012).

Finally, as I mentioned previously, e-mail correspondence is considered personal communication and is not included in your reference sheet. If you quote an email in your paper, cite the source after the quote:

(J. Anders, personal communication, May 6, 2012).

Secondary Sources

Secondary sources are only to be used if a primary sources is not available. Some people call secondary sources a "quote within a quote" where you are using a quote for your paper that contains a quote from another source. For example:

Schott's Original Miscellany (as cited in Humphrey, 2014) says ...

In this case, your reference page would only include the reference for Humphrey. Because you have noted that Humphrey is quoting from Schott's Original Miscellany, you would not add Schott's Original Miscellany to your reference page because you did not get the quote directly from Schott's Original Miscellany.

Classical Works

The APA Manual states that a reference is not necessary for major classical works. Because the dates of these works are often difficult to pin down, the only requirement when referencing or quoting these sources is an in text citation with the name of the original author and the date of the translation you are using. For example, if we were to quote a translation of Plato's Republic, following the quote we would write:
(Plato, trans. 2001).

Religious Texts

Citing the Bible or other religious texts can be confusing. Because the Bible and the Quran texts have standardized in a Book/Chapter/Verse scheme, they can be cited. Here is the general format for your in-text citations. Immediately after a biblical quote: (*Version of the Bible*, Abbreviation of Biblical book. verse start-verse end).

I will make you a great nation, and I will bless you, and make your name great, so that you will be a blessing (*Complete Jewish Bible*, Gen. 12.2).

Alternatively,

…as written in Genesis 12:2 (Complete Jewish Bible).

As long the version of the bible stays the same in future in-text citations, for any subsequent quotes, simply cite the biblical book, chapter and verse. (Gen. 11.6-12.8).
For a proper reference, simply write:

Complete Jewish Bible. Ed. Bill Johnson. New York: Baker House, 2012.
Print.

Unidentified Author or Anonymous Author

Sometimes a work has an unidentified author or anonymous author. In these cases, the work is cited differently than a work with no author. For the in text citation, simply list the title of the work (whether a book, article, chapter, etc.) in quotations followed by the year of publication: ("Shooting Stars", 2007). For anonymous authors, simply cite (Anonymous, 2010). When including an anonymous reference on your reference page, list the reference by alphabetical order according to the word Anonymous.

Where to Put Quotation Marks and Punctuation

This is one of those extemely detailed formatting features of APA style that most students miss. There are strict rules depending on the kind of quotation or paraphrase that you are using. Let's go through the most common forms here:

A Direct Quote - 40 Words or Less

If you are using a direct quote, put the direct quote in quotations. If the quote is 40 words or less, include the quote within the paragraph you are writing. After your quote is completed, enclose it with a double quotation mark followed immediately by the in text citation, then a comma (if the quote is part of another sentence), or a period (if the quotation ends a sentence). Either way, the punctuation is never after the quotation. It always follows the in text citation.

In text citations are never followed by quotation marks.

A Direct Quote - Greater than 40 Words

If your direct quote is great than 40 words, it should be freestanding and indented a half inch as a block quote. Whenever using a block quote, do not use quotation marks. Quotation marks are used to separate your writing from a quote. However, because block quotes are freestanding, we do not need them for longer quotes. Finally, the punctuation in a block quote follows the last word of the quote. The in text citation is then noted after the final punctuation mark.

Citing and Referencing "A Quote Within A Quote"

Have you ever quoted material that cites or quotes another work within your quote? Or have you ever wanted to use a quote that another has used in their book? Here are few pointers to remember in this circumstance. If you are using an original quote found in another work, simply use the in-text citation for the original quote, and the text you have in hand would be used on a reference page.

For example, let's say that the book you have in hand was written by John Smith, and John Smith writes something like:

For those reasons, Goodall notes various reasons why "gorillas become more aggressive at night" (Goodall, 1968).

If you are using the quote "gorillas become more aggressive at night" in your paper, you could write it like this:

Goodall notes that "gorillas become more aggressive at night" (as cited in Smith, 2005).

Closing Thoughts

When I began working on this book in November of 2013, my first thought was, "There are so many questions about how to write references in APA, why hasn't anyone written a book like this?" Now, after just completing the book, I now know why no one has written this book! In one sense, this book was written with a sense of urgency and purpose. Everyday, when I grade college level papers and answer questions online, I see students struggling to get this aspect of APA style right. On the other hand, there were many days where everything began to blur and all of these references blurred into one. All that to say, now that the first version is completed, please be gracious if you see any errors, and feel free to notify me personally so that I can get them fixed. I am relying on you, the academic community, to help make this book perfect. As a gift for helping me, I will gladly send you a free copy of the revised (and fixed) version.

In between writing these kinds of books and teaching, I have been developing a website to help with APA formatting at www.YouVersusTheWorld.com. There, you can download free APA formatted templates for Microsoft Word 2010, 2013, 2011 for Mac, and Apple's Pages '09. You can also find answers to your questions on adding proper headings to your paper, writing advice, and help with research. In the meantime, I am always available to you personally. If you have a question about a reference that is not covered in this book, my personal email address is scott@APAMadeEasy.com - don't hesitate to write with questions, concerns, or suggestions!

Finally, thank you for your support of this book - I really do appreciate it.

Sincerely,

Scott Matkovich
Southern New Hampshire University

Checklist for the Reference Page

- ☑ Your reference page should be on its own page, separate from the text of your paper.
- ☑ References are listed in alphabetical order according to the author's last name. If a reference doesn't have an author, list according to editor's last name. If a reference has neither an author nor editor, list according to the first main word of the title.
- ☑ The word "References" should be written at the top of the page and centered (do not italicize, bold, underline, or use quotations).
- ☑ The reference page should be set to double spaced as with the rest of your paper.
- ☑ Use only 1 space in between all punctuation on your reference page.
- ☑ When citing a source, the first line should not be indented. If your citation falls onto a second or third line, those lines should be indented by hitting the tab key once, or by spacing in 1/2 of an inch. (This is referred to as a hanging indentation).
- ☑ All proper names including the titles of books, author names, companies, etc. should be capitalized.
- ☑ Only the first letter of the title of your reference should be capitalized for web pages, books, chapters, and articles. The only time the first letter should be capitalized in a title is when it includes a proper name or for any journal article (i.e. APA made easy). The same rule applies to subtitles (i.e. APA made easy: Formatting your paper for professional writing).
- ☑ Only spell out the authors' last name. Their first name and middle initial use only the first letter.
- ☑ For references with multiple authors, always keep the order the same as they are listed on the publication.
- ☑ If you are referencing multiple pages, use "pp.". If you are only citing one

page use "p.". The only time you should not use this is with regards to referencing Magazine Articles.

☑ Make sure to include any source that you assigned an in-text citation in the body of your paper.

☑ The APA warns against using Wiki's as a resource for any scholarly paper. Before using a wiki reference, check with your instructor.

☑ Email correspondence is not included in your reference sheet. If you quote an email in your paper, cite the source after the quote: (J. Anders, personal communication, May 6, 2012).

☑ If you quote the Bible or a religious text in your paper, the proper reference should look like this:

Complete NIV Bible. Ed. Bill Johnson. New York: Baker House, 2012. Print.

☑ Your references should include enough detailed information so that the reader can find the source on their own if they wish.

☑ For two or more authors, be sure to make use of the ampersand (&) before the name of the last author.

☑ Book references always begin with the Authors Last Name followed by their first initial and middle initial. However, if the book does not have a stated author or editor, then the reference begins with with the title of the book in italics.

☑ Never use a period after a doi number or URL in a reference.

Made in the USA
San Bernardino, CA
28 January 2020

63708561R10146